THE GREATEST CRIME MYSTERIES OF ALL TIME

THE MADELEINE McCANN CASE
THE JOHN F KENNEDY CASE
THE JACK THE RIPPER CASE

ANDREW GORDON FREW

2017

INTRODUCTION

The purpose of this book sets out from the first to solve the Madeleine McCann case. This work has come at the tail end of a busy year which has seen the release of two of my other investigative crime books,. I set out to complete a trilogy of works, this year, which revolved around the genre of crime.

Glancing over the manuscript again, I can say it looks still a little raw, the thrills are lacking and the peripheries of the work, that gives its literary status falls short but in the end this may pay to its advantage for the reader, who wants to read a very quick resolution.

In dealing with this crime, I necessarily am handicapped I don't have State resources or the man power, but this pays its own reward, for I am under no obligation to account for my time, so I am able to tread paths, pass down routes, spend time on speculating the improbable scenario's that others are unable due to financial factors and accountability. Therefore I have been freed to investigate the improbable route in my calculations to resolve this mystery. That is what it remains to this day and the very reason why on this tenth anniversary of her abduction this work completes the last of my trilogy of books on crimes of the century. It takes its place with pride with the other subject matters I have dealt with these being the assassination of John F Kennedy to uncovering the identity of Jack the Ripper the first and second works of this trilogy. I first heard of the McCann case ten years ago, like everybody else was shocked by this sad story, the tale of a pretty girl who had from the first huge public interest, and how the parents used it, understandably to their advantage to find Madeleine. But alas, ten years later and there is still no resolution to the crime.

So now the case falls under my remit for solving the unsolvable those cases where there are no clues, no leads to go on, that makes the case a riddle, an enigma, and in the minds of the public an unsolvable case, that will fade into the crime annals. That the next generation of researches will take for subject matter to a weary public.

A resolution to a crime is more probable in the first few hours or days of time lapsed, the less likely as years pass or a decade, but there are still clues that can be had, that through the passing of time can be revealed, sometimes through advances in crime identification and in other clues that emerge in new documents that suddenly become available, as in the release of the new JFK files. It is not my intention to go over the statements of those involved or to incriminate people closely connected with the case. I take a more unconventional approach examining Madeleine McCann. Who is the subject of this book, this crime the pivotal centre of this my investigation. Though only three years at the time of her abduction she left enough trace from clues in her early life for me to investigate. That really is the subject of this book, her work.

We will be examining or looking at her art work to resolve this case, those drawings her mother keeps on her wall to this very day, to provide the clues that will lead me to the perpetrator of this hideous crime. I have found in the past it is the analysis of the subjects fingerprints a person leaves behind that guides us to a resolution. So we will be looking at Madeleine's art work very closely in this book. Something I am sure all the investigators so far in this case have paid no mind too, rejected that thesis from the start as a waste of resources. As I mentioned, I am under no such burden of accountability for time, I am free to think the improbable, think outside the box, be the outsider examine all possibilities that is I, believe, needed when one is dealing with a case such as this, a mystery that is becoming the missing person crime of our century. But this is not how I would like it to remain, we want to find Madeleine, take her out of the crime box she been placed.

The objective of this work be in no doubt is to find Madeleine McCann the means at my disposal are two-fold. Firstly I pace the reader through her art work, that can be an odd place to start, but it her fingerprint of herself she left behind, her recognisable image. Our fingerprints never change no matter how old we get, the leopard, so to speak never changes its spots. Now in the case of her the art work of the child will be expressed I have no doubt in her later life.

Detectives applying their search for her on the basis of finding Madeleine's, art work I would say is doubtful this is where true crime researchers come in and apply their trade. Documents once unobtainable are now available on the internet, making the search all that less time consuming, yet when one is still dealing with a needle in a hay stack you need a place to start. This is where thinking outside the box is a must which comes to my second scenario the thought process of where to start the hunt.

For me the place of the abduction is the least place I would look, though obvious to investigators and the like, yet if there was even a little clue, they would've found it by now, with all the massive resources they have had at their disposal. No, I begin, by deduction of the facts from the purpose of the crime, which in essence was a means to acquire a child. Not to kill a child, not to sell a child, but to acquire a child. This fact tells me that Madeleine is alive, even now. Our search then is not in vain, which takes me to the second scenario, the child taken was of an age not predicted, Madeleine's siblings were a much better alternative to a kidnapper that wanted to bring a child up from the very beginning, the bond would be stronger.

But, in this case a three year old was taken this tells me the kidnapper, she desired a replacement for a lost child.

I believe this being the case, the woman I have no doubt, drawing least attention too, authorities would travel as far away from Praia as possible yet remain on Portugal's territory. This takes me to Lagos harbour I believe then via boat to the Azores Islands a group of Isles off the Portugal coast. It is in one of these small Islands Madeleine will be found. I begin my search, I will find her there and this book is proof of that. Do not be astonished, for an old adage says, where none has looked there you find me.

Author

THE MADELEINE McCANN CASE

MADELEINE Aged 3

BACKGROUND

Madeleine Beth McCann (born 12 May 2003) disappeared on the evening of 3 May 2007 from her bed in a holiday apartment in Praia da Luz, a resort in the Algarve region of Portugal, sparking what one newspaper called "the most heavily reported missing-person case in modern history". Her whereabouts remain unknown.

Madeleine was on holiday from the UK with her parents, Kate and Gerry McCann, her two-year-old twin siblings, and a group of family friends and their children. She and the twins had been left asleep at 20:30 in the ground-floor apartment, while the McCann's and friends dined in a restaurant 55 metres (180 ft) away. The parents checked on the children throughout the evening, until Madeleine's mother discovered she was missing at 22:00. Over the following weeks, particularly after misinterpreting a British DNA analysis, the Portuguese police came to believe that Madeleine had died in an accident in the apartment, and that her parents had covered it up. The McCann's were given arguido (suspect) status in September 2007, which was lifted when Portugal's attorney general archived the case in July 2008 because of a lack of evidence.

The parents continued the investigation using private detectives until Scotland Yard opened its own inquiry, Operation Grange, in 2011. The senior investigating officer announced that he was treating the disappearance as "a criminal act by a stranger", most likely a planned abduction or burglary gone wrong. In 2013 Scotland Yard released e-fit images of men they wanted to trace, including one of a man seen carrying a child toward the beach that night. Shortly after this the Portuguese police reopened their inquiry. Operation Grange was scaled back in 2015, but the remaining detectives continued to pursue a small number of inquiries described in April 2017 as significant.

The disappearance attracted sustained international interest and saturation coverage in the UK reminiscent of the death of Diana in 1997. The McCann's were subjected to intense scrutiny and baseless allegations of involvement in their daughter's death, particularly in the tabloid press and on Twitter. In 2008 they and their travelling companions received damages and apologies from Express Newspapers, and in 2011 the McCann's testified before the Leveson Inquiry into British press misconduct, lending support to those arguing for tighter press regulation.

Kate and Gerry McCann holding a photo of Madeleine, of how, she could look now.

CHAPTER ONE	PRAIA DA LUZ
CHAPTER TWO	FIRST CLUE
CHAPTER THREE	THE TYPE OF SEARCH
CHAPTER FOUR	THE ART OF MADELEINE
CHAPTER FIVE	HOTEL DO COLEGIO
CHAPTER SIX	CHILDREN'S PLAY ROOM
CHAPTER SEVEN	MOTHER, I AM HERE
CHAPTER EIGHT	THE MESSAGE FROM MADELEINE

CHAPTER ONE

PRAIA DA LUZ

We are now going to investigate this case and make no mistake we are going to find Madeleine McCann. The search will take us into unknown territory we are going to think outside the box, and into the mind of the person, or persons connected with the abduction and to a very remarkable end, I leave the reader to make up his mind. But first we begin at the beginning a very good place to start and to the very place of her disappearance in the holiday apartment Rua Dr Agostinho da Silva, Praia da Luz, a resort in the Algarve region of Portugal.

10am: The sixth day of the McCann's week-long holiday in the Algarve. The couple place their daughter, Madeleine and her twin siblings, Sean and Amelie, in the Ocean Club's Kids Club while they go for a walk.

12.30pm: After collecting the children, Kate and Gerry head to their apartment, 5a, on ground floor of block five of the Waterside Village Gardens, for lunch before going to the Ocean Club swimming pool.

2.29pm: This photograph of Madeleine is taken at the pool. It is last photograph, she looks really happy.

3.30pm: Children return to Kids Club.

5.30pm: Children eat dinner at Kids Club.

6pm: Kate takes children back to apartment while Gerry goes to an hour-long tennis lesson.

6.30pm: Gerry asks David Payne, one of the so-called "tapas seven", to check on Kate and the children at the apartment.

7pm: Gerry returns to the apartment and the children are put to bed in the front bedroom overlooking the car park and beyond it, the street. Madeleine is placed in the single bed nearest the door. There is an empty bed against the opposite wall beneath the window. Between the two beds are two travel cots containing the twins.

7.30pm: The McCann's shower and change.

8pm: The couple share a bottle of wine together.

8.35pm: The McCann's are the first of the group to arrive at the tapas restaurant, 50 yards away from their apartment.

8.55pm: The group has ordered starters when the routine of checking on the children begins. Matt Oldfield goes to check his own apartment. He also tells the Paynes, who are still in their apartment, that the group is waiting for them at the restaurant.

9.05pm: Gerry returns to the apartment through the unlocked patio doors to check on the children. Earlier that week, the McCanns had used a key to go in through the front door next to the children's bedroom but, worrying the noise might wake the children, they began using the patio doors, leaving them unlocked.

He enters the apartment and sees that the children's bedroom door, which they always left slightly ajar, is now open to 45 degrees. Thinking this is odd, he glances into his own bedroom to see if Madeleine has gone into her parents' bed. But he sees that all three are still fast asleep where the McCanns left them. Putting the door back to five degrees, he went to the toilet and then returned to the restaurant. This is the last time he would see his daughter.

9.08pm: Gerry sees Jeremy Wilkins, another holidaymaker at the resort, on the opposite side of the road as he walks back to the tapas bar and crosses over to talk. Wilkins and his partner are eating in their apartment since their youngest child will not settle. The two men spend several minutes talking.

9.10pm: Jane Tanner walks up the road, unnoticed by Gerry and Wilkins, although she sees them. She spots a man walking quickly across the top of the road in front of her, going away from the apartment block and heading to the outer road of the resort complex. He is carrying a sleeping girl in pink pyjamas who is hanging limply in his arms. The sighting is odd, but hardly exceptional in a holiday resort. Her daughter is fine; Tanner returns to the table.

9.30pm: Kate gets up to make next check on her children but Matthew Oldfield and Russell O'Brien are checking, too. Oldfield offers to check the McCann's children.

In the McCann's apartment, Oldfield notices the children's bedroom door is open again, but this means little to him. He merely observes all is quiet and makes a cursory glance inside the room seeing the twins in their cot, but not directly seeing Madeleine's bed from the angle at which he stood. Afterwards, he could not say for sure if she had been there or not. Nor could he say if the window and shutter had been open.

He would later get a hard time from the police because of this. During his interviews, he was aggressively accused of taking Madeleine, coming under suspicion because he had offered to take Kate's turn.

10.00pm: Kate checks on the children. She becomes alarmed when she reaches out to the children's bedroom door and it blows shut. Inside the room, the window is open and the shutter is up. The twins are sleeping but Madeleine's bed is empty.

Shortly after 10pm: Rachael Oldfield goes to Tanner's apartment to tell her Madeleine has been taken. Tanner says: "Oh my God. I saw a man carrying a girl."

10.15pm: Oldfield goes down to the 24-hour reception at the bottom of the hill to raise the alarm. Police are called.

10.30pm: Local police are first to arrive on the scene.

Holiday apartment Rua Dr Agostinho da Silva, Praia da Luz,

On the evening of May 3rd, she vanished from this apartment, where she had been sleeping with her brother and sister, twins in block 5a, lower floor. The McCann's were on a seven-night spring break at the two-bedroom, ground-floor apartment

The apartment is on the edge of travel firm Mark Warner's Ocean Club. The Ocean Club is one of several collections of tourist accommodation in the popular holiday town, which is located close to the larger town of Lagos, about an hour's drive from Faro airport. The McCann's were on a seven-night spring break at the two-bedroom, ground-floor apartment

It would be necessary for the perpetrator to get away as quickly as possible on the quickest route. The car used in kidnapping Madeleine would be temporary, a rent-a-car, for it is certain to commit such a crime the perpetrator does not live on this resort. This map shows the main road routes in and out of the resort. The important route is the N125 it takes you east in the direction heading to Lagos. It is about a 5 mile drive.

We arrive at Lagos harbour and there is I believe a boat is waiting to take delivery of Madeleine. This act implies there are now two perpetrators involved. The rent-a –car is delivered back and Madeleine, who is still in heavy sleep is taken aboard the waiting boat. Madeleine must have been under a sleeping dose, which she could only awaked from next morning in her new home. I cannot prove this but there must have been a reason she raised no alarm.

Lagorent in Lagos

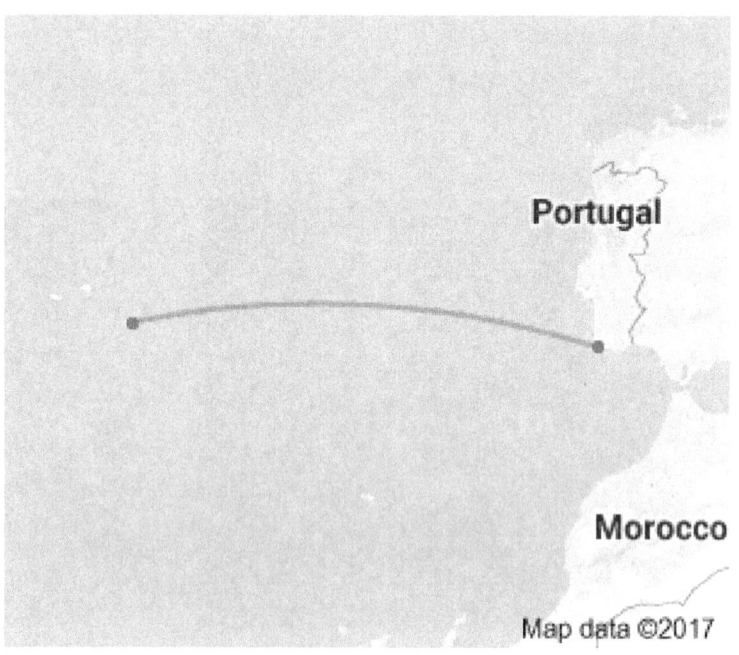

The boat leaves for its destination as far away as possible to a place to hide Madeleine. This location would still be part of Portugal but far from its land base YET IS STILL PART OF ITS TERRITORY. This would take the boat to the Azores in the mid Atlantic.

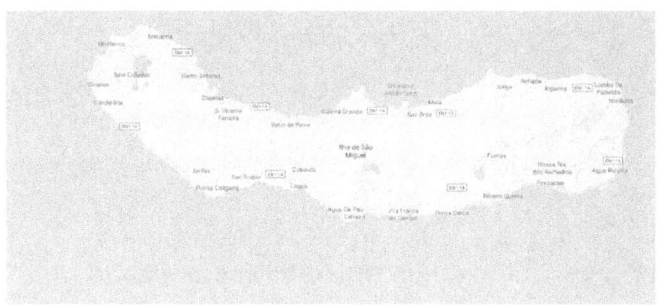

São Miguel Island

São Miguel Island also referred to locally as "The Green Island", is the largest and most populous island in the Portuguese archipelago of the Azores. It is also the easiest to reach being the nearest Island to mainland Portugal.

That is 1,484 km distance from Lagos to São Miguel Island. They arrive by night by boat and dock on its main harbour, Ponta Delgada. A car waits to take Madeleine to her final destination her home on the Isle.

Ponta Delgada

CHAPTER TWO

FIRST CLUE

There are over 592 Hotels on São Miguel Island, all of them a prime suspect for the location of Madeleine. I believe that she is alive in one of these Isle Hotel complexes. But my gut feeling draws me to the twenty three Hotels located in its main harbour, Ponta Delgada, the capitol of São Miguel.

I have no need to visit the locations on site they are fully documented on the internet through travel brochures. This has given me the inside view window I need for what I am searching for the clue too Madeleine.

My eye was caught by a logo that I found in Hotel do Colegio, the Hotel laying back from the main harbour in Ponta Delgada.

THE LOGO IN HOTEL DO COLEGIO

Why it was this logo that caught my eye is maybe obvious to any of my readers that have avidly followed the Madeleine case. This logo reminded me of Madeleine with her twin siblings, yes all dancing together. A gut feeling told me to take a closer look.

MADELEINE WITH YOUNGER TWIN BROTHER AND SISTER

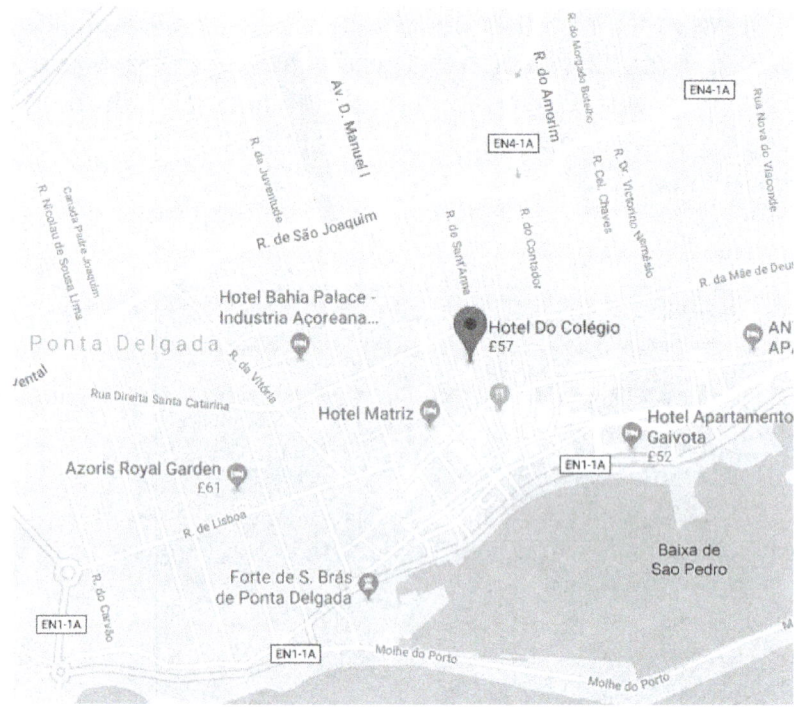

Located in the heart of Ponta Delgada, Hotel do Colegio is within a 10-min walk of Ponta Delgada Harbour and University of the Azores.

CHAPTER THREE

THE TYPE OF SEARCH

I am searching for Madeleine's drawings from when she was a toddler expressed in the refurbishment of this Hotel do Colegio, a secret way for her to send an S.O.S call without raising suspicion from her captors.

While investigating for such evidence it is not to be expected that the walls of this Hotel will be marked, 'HELP, MADELEINE I AM HERE.' That would be crude in the extreme and certainly the captor would not allow it, she would be watchful at all times.

I say 'she,' for the first time that is the sex I believe masterminded the disappearance of Madeleine. Not to be controversial, this very fact is good news, if there any good news about this kidnapping at all, I feel the prime motive for this crime is child loss, a replacement for a dead child with another, a motive that would keep Madeleine alive.

The question now is, why Madeleine. She has a distinctive right eye feature, which I believe supports a theory, that the child of the captor also had this feature in the eye. If it was the case that the motherless child just wanted any child then she would've chosen one of Madeleine's siblings, the opportunity was there, but because of this similar feature it was her that was wanted.

The family photos of the residence these specific identifications are clues to look for among all the items displayed in any hotel. But most important of all it is Madeleine's art work as the child she once was where we shall find our clue on her whereabouts. Her art at home as a child known only by her mother and father the McCann family.

Memories are the link between past and future. How many of those memories are still remembered by Madeleine, and how clearly, we do not know, much of this link is forgotten with age, but Madeleine was a very mature in age four year old when she vanished. She could sing and draw and in her nature was very independent ahead of her four years. Those early memories she could've retained even now as a teenager.

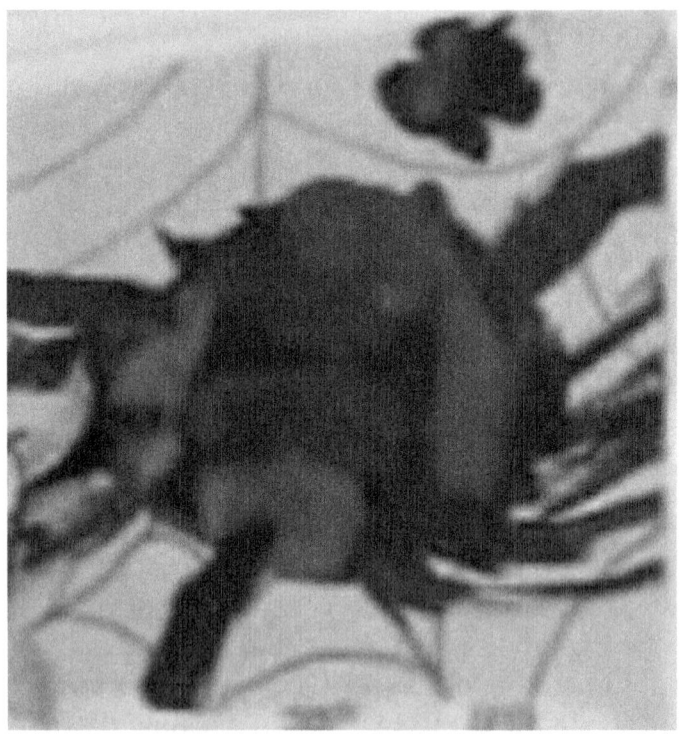

CAUGHT IN A SPIDERS WEB

CHAPTER FOUR

THE ART OF MADELEINE

At this stage of the book it has been all theory, and nothing factually substantial, we are still far away from our goal to find Madeleine. Like a hound dog that follows the scent of an item to go on, I needed clues from Madeleine herself, the things she left behind so I scanned her home life.

A photo clip from a rare You Tube video Mrs McCann shows off Madeleine's work.

MADELEINE'S ART WORK AT AGE 3

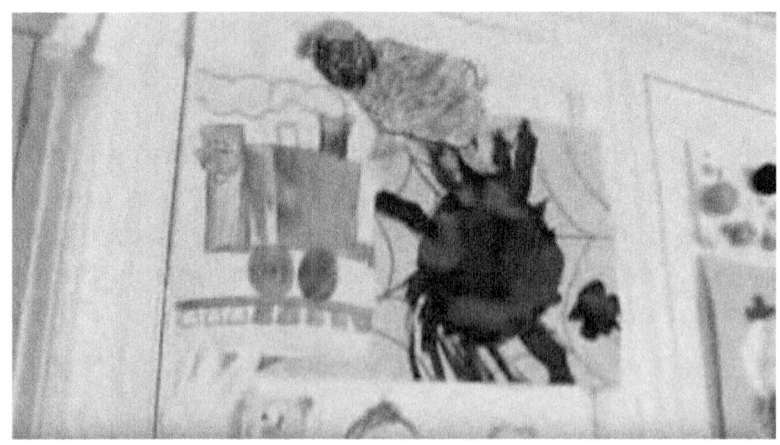

Drawings of a train on its tracks, the spider in a web and above an animal like a lamb as in Christ the Lamb of God.

From Left to right a rabbit face, a teddy face and a picture inscribed 'Our family.'

A person with hat and scarf also seven stars divided into six coloured stars below the name of Madeleine. There is also a picture with the number five, in the circle.

These paintings by Madeleine are kept in the same formation on the wall since the day Madeleine vanished as a shrine to her memory. Madeleine herself would daily of looked up at them enshrined them in her memory. This was her work the placement of them would have been imprinted in her. The average age of the first "explicit" (or episodic) memory that can be recalled by an adult is not until about three-and-a-half years old, on average. Along with these drawings Madeline would remember her loving mother and father. When she grew older she would recall them. As of 2017, she now being 13, memories of a previous life must still flash in her mind, must mean something, but how to communicate them.

These paintings are the clues I am looking for her they reveal her psychological trace. They are unique to her alone and as I, hope she does, she will trace again these drawings, in exact alignment in her other world environment if given the opportunity

CHAPTER FIVE

HOTEL DO COLEGIO

We are on São Miguel Island, Azores. and we are going to pay a visit, to Hotel do Colegio. Nobody knows our intent, for all is as it should be, like Holmes in disguise we will make a thorough search around. We are going to take a look inside through travel brochures. These will give an inside view window for what I am searching for the toddler drawings leading to Madeleine.

We travel down a cobbled road we follow the street leading us to Hotel do Colegio. I with anticipation feel nervous for this could lead to solving the greatest missing case this century the rediscovery of Madeleine.

HOTEL DO COLEGIO

After refurbishment and new paint work in 2017

On one of the tables inside the hotel I found this collection of memories laid out.

'A distinctive right eye feature, which I believe supports a theory, that the child of the captor also had this feature in the eye.'

NOTICE THE DISTINCTIVE MARK OF THE PUPIL IN THE LEFT EYE

Honey comb like public area

The Pool area and at the back is the children's play area

Hotel do Colegio

Children's play room the place I begin my search

I am drawn to this area, the children's play area for clues for evidence that Madeleine is here. The photos are published in 2017 after the recent refurbishment of the Hotel.

CHAPTER SIX

CHILDREN'S PLAY ROOM

We are going to enter into the play room, I have two photos one showing the front of the room the other the back. All sides of the room is covered by these two photos. The photos were taken by commission by tripe advisor. I assume an independent professional service used for advertising the facilities of the hotel. Now what we see in the room, is what you would expect in a children's play room. At first I thought there was nothing here to give me clues to the whereabouts of Madeleine but through the arrangement of the items in the room I could see, what she, yes Madeleine who I believe arranged the room has done. She has sent a message to her parents. I drew back, not believing what I was witnessing.

I could see her art fingerprint in this room that she had done in her young life, those drawings that Mrs McCann keeps of her for memory sake as a shrine on the wall at her home. Here they are replicated in this children's play room. Each item imitating what she remembered when she was four.

The Children's play room facing windows at Hotel do Colegio

Mrs McCann showing Madeleine's drawings

Mrs McCann points to a train, Madeleine drew her last picture before she vanished. The train, is placed in the play room area.

Madeline drew a teddy (central). In the room we see teddy book below on table. A head with 'Our family.' written above it. We see below a book with a name above. The rabbit is not in this room but left out because the next room is a lounge area.

Yellow cab on table used in kidnap

On the ceiling there is a light above the Hotel do Colegio plaques and the train.

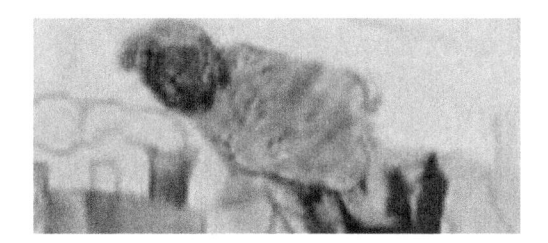

Situated above the spider and the train in her drawing is a lamb, representing the lamb of God, Christ the light of the world.

CHAPTER SEVEN

MOTHER, I AM HERE

The placement of items within the room is in accordance with the arrangement of her art, only her Mother would've, known this or anyone analysing her art on You Tube.

Police work deals with factual evidence, I understand this, but this is a very unusual case, and is necessarily handicapped by no clues, thus the crime becomes a riddle, an enigma that cannot ever be unravelled.

If Police evidence is factual we must give what is needed and return to the children's play room. The one fact everybody agrees is that Madeleine was taken on 3. 5. 2007. Make a note of all these numbers carefully for they are inscribed within the play room.

On the floor of the room a set of numbers next to it on the table is a jig saw puzzle. It implies us to solve the puzzle on the floor.

We start with the arrow which points to the number 3.

3. Next to it 5.

5. Next to it the number 6 or 9.

9 next row up

We have the number 2. A cat oO then 7

2007

Madeleine was taken on the 3rd day of the 5th month at the 9th hour in the year, 2007

Children's play room looking at door

Madeleine wearing a hat and scarf

The name Madeleine appears above six colours and as we look at the children's play area a blackboard appears above the number 6. She is then on the Black board.

ACORES

Should be spelt Azores the Island group off Portugal. But notice something very significant in a blow up of the blackboard

The A and C are connected with a line. A is the 1st letter of the alphabet and C is the 3rd. The number 13 and below the A is a round face the right eye is marked. There a line that goes to a faded child to a heart.

Madeleine was 13 when she drew this.

CHAPTER EIGHT

THE MESSAGE FROM MADELEINE

I was able to construct her message from a rare video clip showing Madeleine's art. Along with the photos in the brochure of the newly refurbished **Hotel do Colegio.**

Rare FOOTAGE VIDEO OF MADELEINE MCCANN AT HOME :: Madeleine singing & Madeleine Playing .

https://www.youtube.com/watch?v=kSMwuMe1gEI

THE SCENARIO

Madeleine was abducted on the 3rd May 2007, taken from PRAIA da Luz to Lagos and onto Hotel do Colegio on the Island of São Miguel in the Azores. As she grew up she became trusted by her captor. In 2017 a refurbishment of Hotel do Colegio was undertaken. After living with her captor for 10 years Madeleine was entrusted to take part in it and suggested the colour scheme for the frontage of the building. Pleased with Madeleine's colour choice her captor unbeknown to her used the same colour scheme Madeleine had used in a drawing.

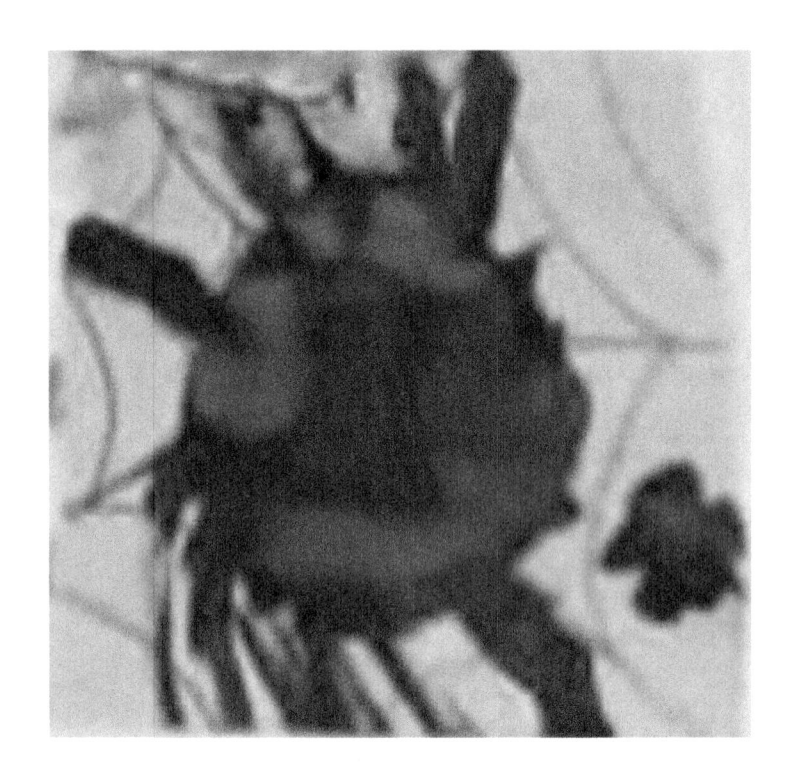

A spider in its web guards its food

Before

Colour scheme now

One day a photographer from Trip Advisor on behest of management decided to visit the Hotel to make professional photos for a brochure to advertise the facilities of this Hotel via the internet. Madeleine arranged it so the play room items in the children's play area followed her art work drawings, using this only opportunity to receive help. The photographs would be seen cross the world. All it would take is somebody who had seen her art work to put it all together.

I will put the items in the Hotel play room side by side with her drawings she done at home so that her message will become crystal clear. That message: I AM HERE.

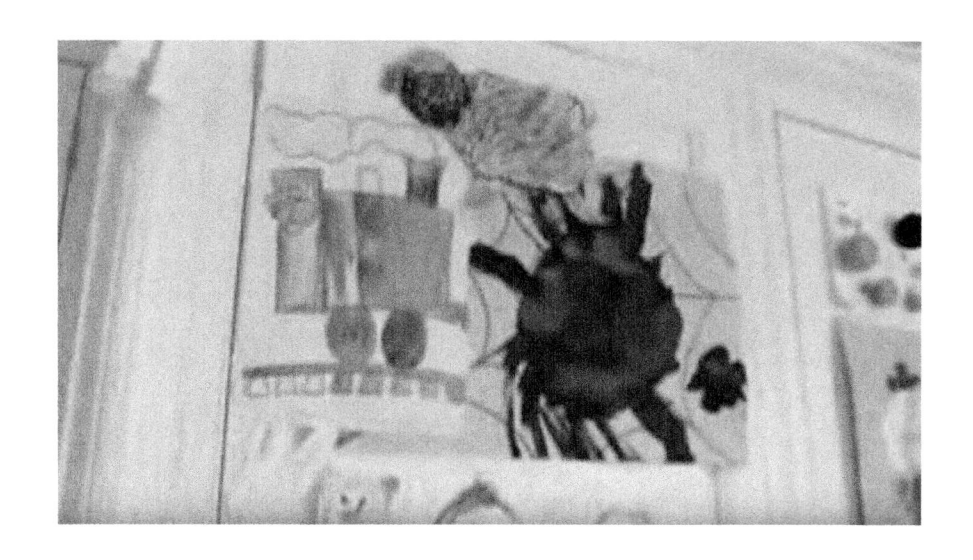

These drawings, covers all items on one side of Hotel children's play room

These drawings, covers all items in other side of Hotel children's play room

Play room

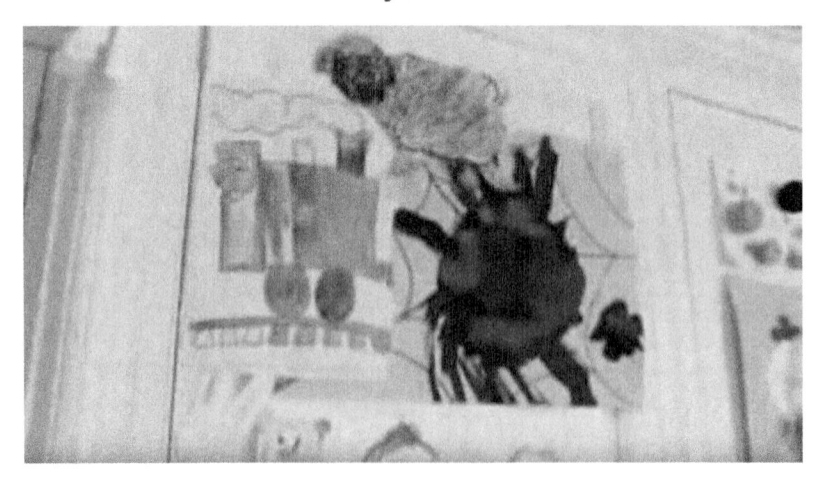

Her drawings

Figure one

Play room

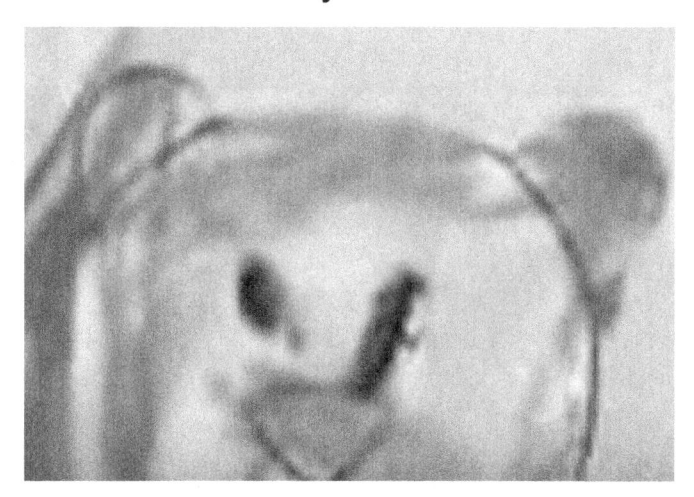

Her drawing

Figure two

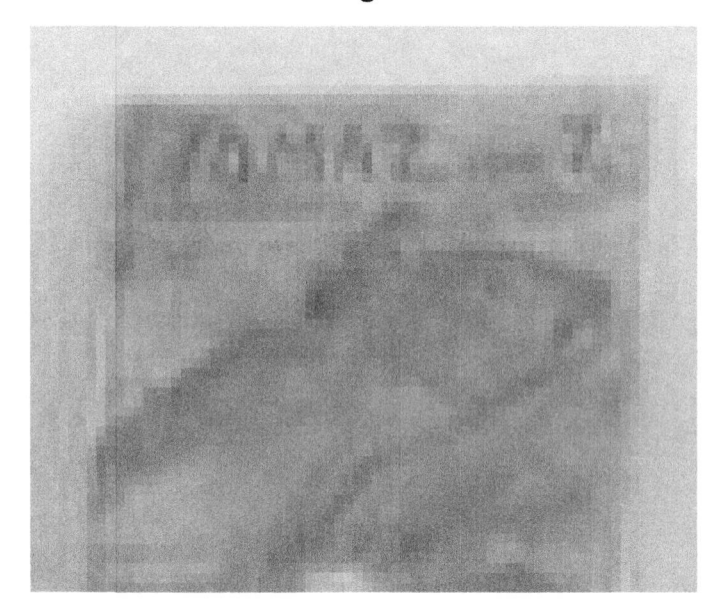

Play room

Her drawing

Figure three

Play room

Her drawing

Figure four

Play room

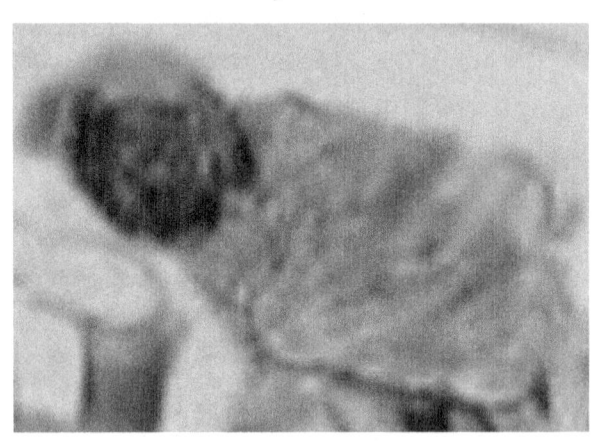

Her drawing

Figure five

Play room hotel plaque

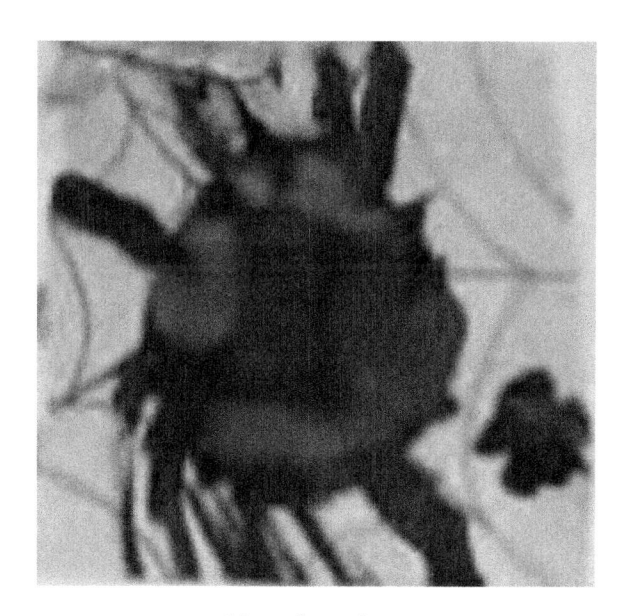

Her drawing

Figure six

Play room

Date Madeleine Vanished

Start at arrow >

3rd Day

5th Month

9th Hour

2007 Year

Her arrangement of floor puzzle

Figure seven

Other side of play room

Her drawing

Figure eight

Play room 5 drawings on pillar

On her drawing wall (5)

Figure nine

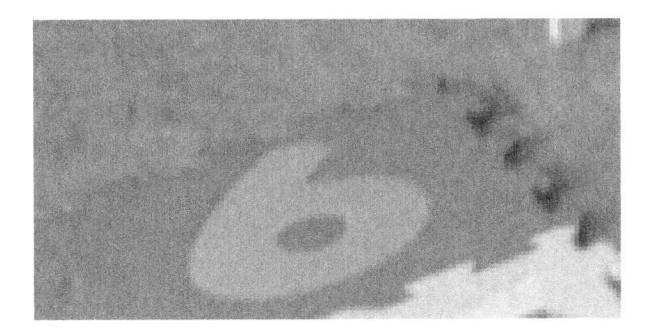

Play room

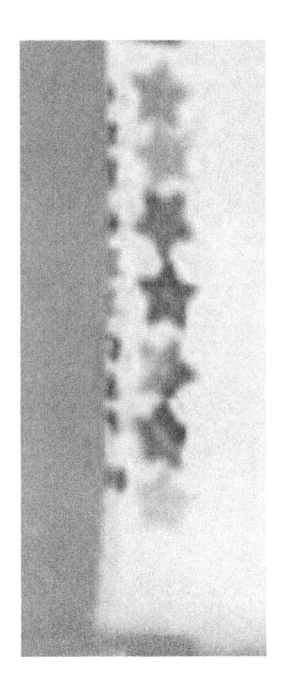

Her stars have six colours

Figure ten (a)

Play room black board

Her name her identification

Figure ten (b)

A round face, and marked right eye, a chalk line to faded child.

A_C connects the first and third letter of alphabet making 13

MADELEINE IS 13. That is early 2017 the date of refurbishment of Hotel.

Figure eleven

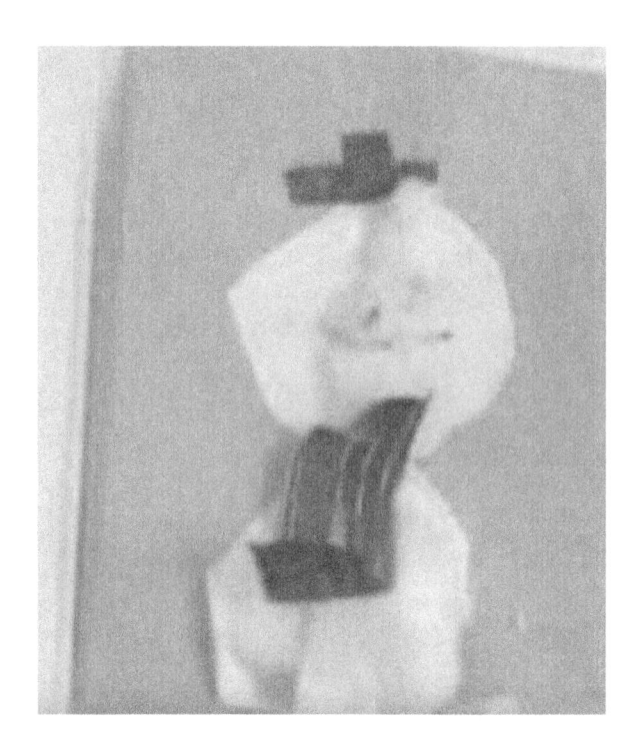

Madeleine's three year old drawing of herself. But Madeleine herself is not found in the children's playroom of the Hotel. So she is telling us to look for her outside and that takes us to the Hotel's pool area.

Figure twelve

Madeleine's art, Mrs McCann, hangs on her wall. Pink- Move clothing so she could be wearing this colour to identify herself in the pool area.

I feel Madeleine is guiding me to find her in this area. So I am going to peruse these pool photographs from the Hotel brochure. I am looking for something, something out of the ordinary, not sure what though, but I will sense it when I see it, she is a captive. Also it might be quite dangerous for her to show herself in this pool area if there are photos being taken, her captor would not allow Madeleine to show her face in them.

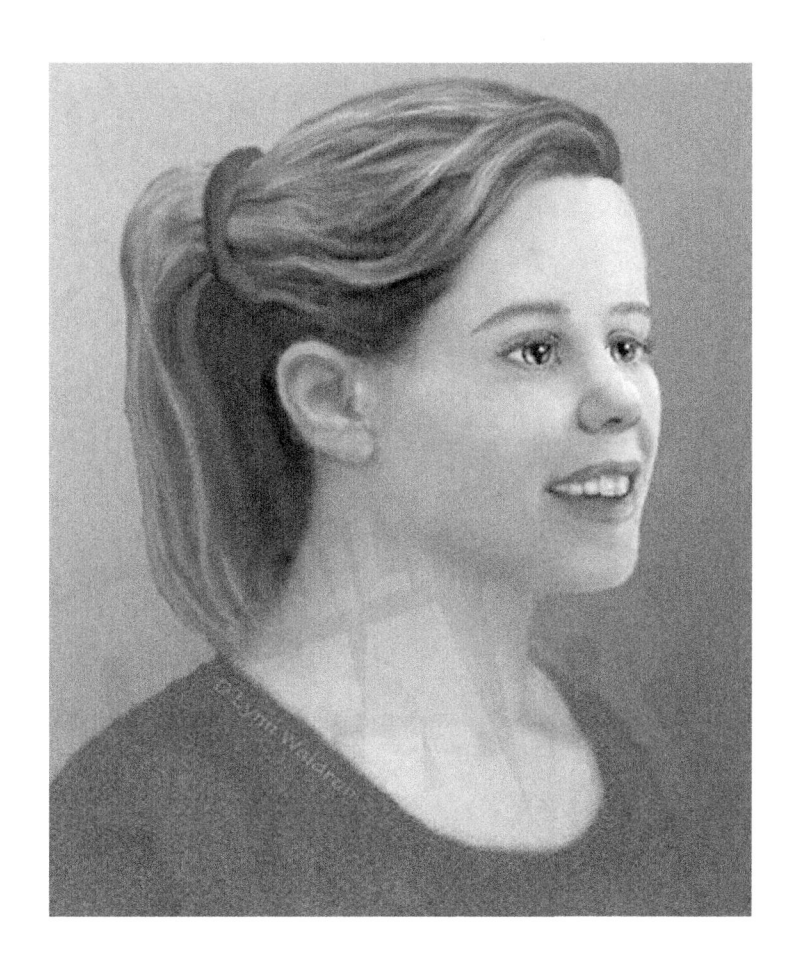

How Madeleine could look now.

Also to help me in my search I have the latest e-fit of what Madeleine could look like now at the age of 13, an age she said she was from A_C children's blackboard.

Outside the pool area sits a woman.

A blow up image of the woman she looks imposing.

Also in the pool area is a girl lying on a sun bed, perhaps it's.......

A blow up image of the girl, no I don't think that's Madeleine. Mind you, we do change with age, but she seems way too serene. I get a strong feeling from the way the clues are left, Madeleine wants out of there now.

Madeleine has led me to a pool, all is here are two people, one older, a mother and daughter perhaps. She is not Madeleine. I am really looking for something convincing and then tenacity was rewarded, my wait was over. Note nobody is behind the pillar

Note also that pool door to the right is shut

Door is shut

Then, the photographer captured the same door opened.

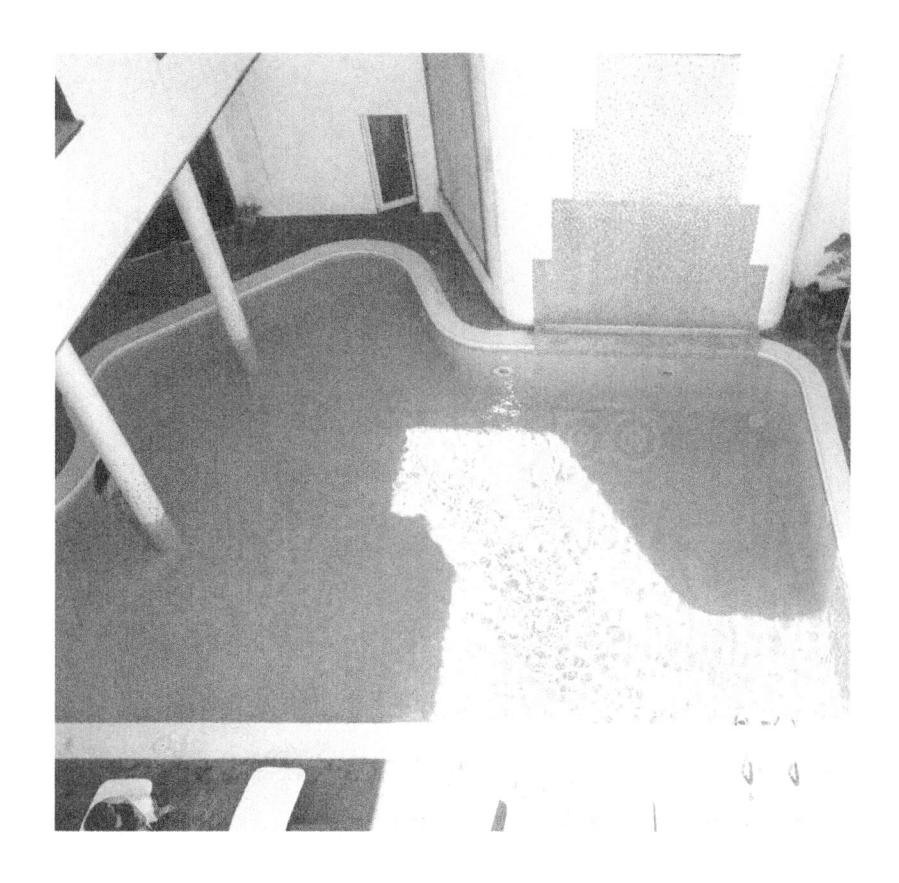

The woman sits at the bottom of the photo she looks at the girl behind the pillar. The door above is ajar she came out off. She just stands behind the pillar. Saying I am **HERE**. I feel that gut feeling that this is something I was waiting for its convincing.

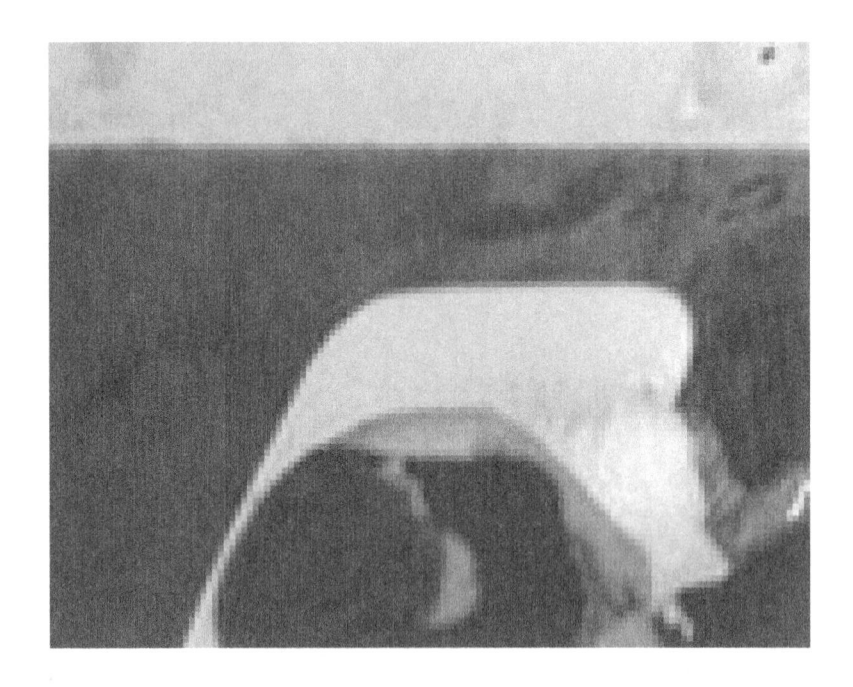

The woman sitting turns her head noticing the girl acting oddly behind the pool pillar.

There is something wrong here. She hides her face, because of the woman (Captor?)

…it's her?

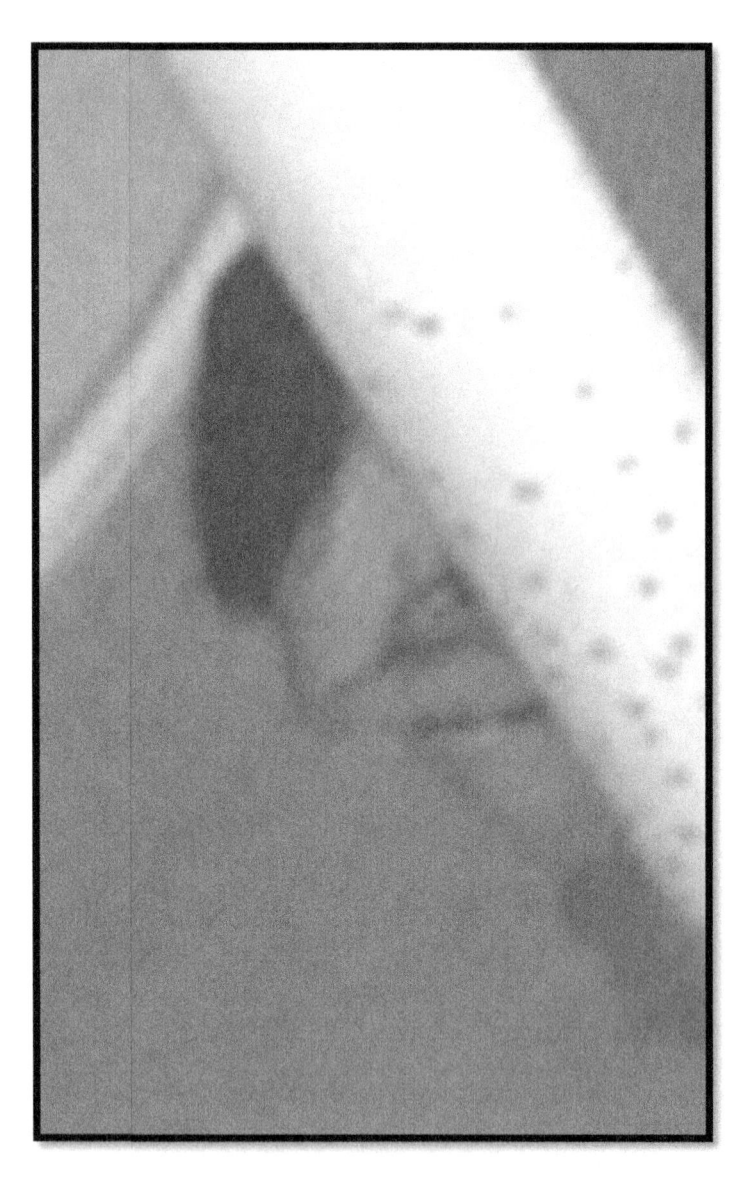

Madeleine McCann?

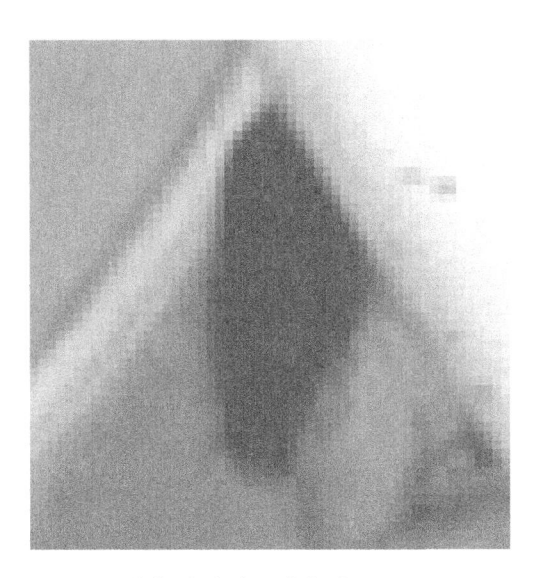

Madeleine McCann

Whoever she is, she the one that placed the clues, that led me here. Her hair looks different from what I expected it's darker, so is her hair found in photo e-fit picture. The colour of her bikini matches her Move-Pink drawing. I think reader, you understand my situation. It could be a hoax this girl is playing tricks the readers can make up their own minds whether this is Madeleine McCann or not.

THE

END

THE
JOHN F KENNEDY CASE

NOTE FROM AUTHOR

November 22nd has become a special day in the annals of history for being the day in full view of the eyes of the world the leader of the free world President John F Kennedy was assassinated executed mercilessly by an unknown assassin. In the opinion of the authorities that established the Warren Commission the man responsible for this tragic act was Lee Harvey Oswald. Who himself was murdered at the hands of an assassin Jack Ruby, a notorious local night club owner. This small volume looks at some common-sense facts, facts captured at the scene on that eventful day. The truth and this is what every reader fascinated by this case, wants to know. Every new generation that investigates this case becomes far removed from the events surrounding that era, and is necessarily handicapped by the passing of time, thus the puzzle becomes a riddle, an enigma within an enigma, and so the assassination can never be unravelled. But there are some facts held in motion, photographic evidence, that tell their own story, for the readers too make up their own minds.

London 2017

BACKGROUND

John Fitzgerald Kennedy (May 29, 1917 – November 22, 1963), commonly referred to by his initials JFK, was an American statesman who served as the 35th President of the United States from January 1961 until his assassination in November 1963. Kennedy served at the height of the Cold War, and much of his presidency focused on managing relations with the Soviet Union.

He was a member of the American Democratic Party who represented Massachusetts in the United States House of Representatives and the United States Senate prior to becoming president.

Kennedy was born in Brookline, Massachusetts, to Joseph P. Kennedy, Sr. and Rose Kennedy. A scion of the Kennedy family, he graduated from Harvard University in 1940 before joining the United States Naval Reserve the following year. During World War II, Kennedy commanded a series of PT boats in the Pacific theater and earned the Navy and Marine Corps Medal for his service. After the war, Kennedy represented Massachusetts's 11th congressional district in the United States House of Representatives from 1947 until 1953. He was subsequently elected to the U.S. Senate and served as the junior Senator from Massachusetts from 1953 until 1960. While serving in the Senate, he published *Profiles in Courage*, which won the Pulitzer Prize for Biography. In the 1960 presidential election, Kennedy narrowly defeated Republican opponent Richard Nixon, who was the incumbent Vice President.

Kennedy's time in office was marked by high tensions with Communist states in the Cold War. He increased the number of American military advisers in South Vietnam by a factor of 18 over President Dwight D. Eisenhower. In April 1961, he authorized a failed joint-CIA attempt to overthrow the Cuban government of Fidel Castro in the Bay of Pigs Invasion. He subsequently rejected plans by the Joint Chiefs of Staff to orchestrate false-flag attacks on American soil in order to gain public approval for a war against Cuba. In October 1962, U.S. spy planes discovered that Soviet missile bases had been deployed in Cuba; the resulting period of tensions, termed the Cuban Missile Crisis, nearly resulted in the breakout of a global thermonuclear conflict. Domestically, Kennedy presided over the establishment of the Peace Corps and supported the Civil Rights Movement, but he was largely unsuccessful in passing his New Frontier domestic policies. Kennedy continues to rank highly in historians' polls of U.S. presidents and with the general public. His average approval rating of 70% is the highest of any president in Gallup's history of systematically measuring job approval.

Jackie Kennedy the wife of JFK

On a sunny afternoon on November 22, 1963, Kennedy was assassinated in Dallas, Texas. Lee Harvey Oswald was arrested for the crime, but he was never prosecuted due to his murder by Jack Ruby two days later. Pursuant to the Presidential Succession Act, Vice President Lyndon B. Johnson was sworn in as president later that day. The FBI and the Warren Commission officially concluded that Oswald was the lone assassin, but various groups believed that Kennedy was the victim of a conspiracy. After Kennedy's death, many of his proposals were enacted, including the Civil Rights Act of 1964 and the Revenue Act of 1964.

The funeral of JFK

CONTENTS

NOTE FROM AUTHOR

CHAPTER ONE -   THE ASSASSINATION

CHAPTER TWO   -   THE RUSH TO HOSPITAL

CHAPTER THREE – THE DIRECTION OF THE SHOTS

CHAPTER FOUR -   ALL DIRECTIONS LEAD TO THE
                  TRIPLE UNDERPASS

CHAPTER FIVE -   THE WITNESSES

CHAPTER SIX -   A VISION TO THE SLAUGHTER

CHAPTER ONE

THE ASSASSINATION

Mr. Kennedy had opened his day in Fort Worth, first with a speech in a parking lot and then at a Chamber of Commerce breakfast. The breakfast appearance was a particular triumph for Mrs. Kennedy, who entered late and was given an ovation.

Then the Presidential party, including Governor and Mrs. Connally, flew on to Dallas, an eight-minute flight. Mr. Johnson, as is customary, flew in a separate plane. The President and the Vice President do not travel together, out of fear of a double tragedy.

At Love Field, Mr. and Mrs. Kennedy lingered for 10 minutes, shaking hands with an enthusiastic group lining the fence. The group called itself "Grassroots Democrats."

Mr. Kennedy then entered his open Lincoln convertible at the head of the motorcade. He sat in the rear seat on the right-hand side. Mrs. Kennedy, who appeared to be enjoying one of the first political outings she had ever made with her husband, sat at his left.

In the "jump" seat, directly ahead of Mr. Kennedy, sat Governor Connally, with Mrs. Connally at his left in another "jump" seat. A Secret Service agent was driving and the two others ran alongside.

Behind the President's limousine was an open sedan carrying a number of Secret Service agents. Behind them, in an open convertible, rode Mr. and Mrs. Johnson and Texas's senior Senator, Ralph W. Yarborough, a Democrat.

The motorcade proceeded uneventfully along a 10-mile route through downtown Dallas, aiming for the Merchandise Mart.

Mr. Kennedy was to address a group of the city's leading citizens at a luncheon in his honor.

In downtown Dallas, crowds were thick, enthusiastic and cheering. The turnout was somewhat unusual for this center of conservatism, where only a month ago Adlai E. Stevenson was attacked by a rightist crowd. It was also in Dallas, during the 1960 campaign, that Senator Lyndon B. Johnson and his wife were nearly mobbed in the lobby of the Baker Hotel.

Reception at Dallas

As the motorcade neared its end and the President's car moved out of the thick crowds onto Stennonds Freeway near the Merchandise Mart, Mrs. Connally recalled later, "we were all very pleased with the reception in downtown Dallas."

Reception at Dallas

As Mrs. Connally recalled later, the President's car was almost ready to go underneath a "triple underpass beneath three streets--Elm, Commerce and Main--when the first shot was fired.

At 12:30 o'clock, reports the Warren Commission, Jacqueline Kennedy "heard a sound similar to a motorcycle noise and a cry from Governor Connally, which caused her to look to her right. On turning, she saw a quizzical look on her husband's face as he raised his left hand to his throat.

The first shot hits the throat of the President as shown in frame 230 from the Zapruder film.

"Governor Connally testified that he recognized the first noise as a rifle shot, and the thought immediately crossed his mind that it was an assassination attempt. From his position in the right jump seat immediately in front of the President, he instinctively turned to his right because the shot appeared to come from over his right shoulder. Unable to see the President as he turned, the Governor started to look back over his left shoulder, but he never completed the turn because he felt something strike him in the back.

Governor Connally is hit by second bullet. Zapruder film

"Mrs. Connally, too, heard a frightening noise from her right. Looking back over her right shoulder, she saw that the President had both hands at his neck. She watched as he slumped down with an empty expression on his face. [Secret Service Agent] Roy Kellerman, in the right front seat of the limousine, heard a report like a firecracker. Turning to his right in the direction of the noise, Kellerman heard the President say, 'My God, I am hit.'

"Mrs. Connally heard a second shot fired and pulled her husband down into her lap. Observing his blood-covered chest as he was pulled into his wife's lap, Governor Connally believed himself mortally wounded.

He cried out: 'Oh, no, no, no. My God, they are going to kill us all.' At first Mrs. Connally thought that her husband had been killed, but then she noticed an almost imperceptible movement and knew that he was still alive. She said, 'It's all right. Be still.' The Governor was lying with his head on his wife's lap when he heard a shot hit the President. At that point, both Governor and Mrs. Connally observed brain tissue splattered over the interior of the car."

Zapruder film

Zapruder film

Jackie Kennedy climbing over the back of the Presidential car. Some have thought that she was trying to escape by scrambling over the back of the vehicle after the shooting, in fact she is retrieving a fragment of skull blown out of her husband's head.

Another photo taken by Jim Altgens, a few seconds after the fatal shot struck President Kennedy. Secret Service agent Clint Hill has jumpedonto the back bumper of the limousine to aid Jacqueline Kennedy. The motorcade's "lead car", with Dallas Police Chief Jesse Curry driving, can be seen just ahead of the limo on Elm Street, brakes applied.

The limousine with the fatally wounded President is seen here just west of the Triple Underpass, quickly approaching the ramp leading to Stemmons Freeway. This fascinating photo, taken by bystander Mel McIntire, shows the Book Depository in the background

Note the time--"12:30"--being displayed on the large "Hertz" sign atop the Texas School Book Depository.

CHAPTER TWO

THE RUSH TO HOSPITAL

Rush to Parkland Hospital

Dr. Perry, the first physician to treat the President, said a number of resuscitative measures had been attempted, including oxygen, anesthesia, an indotracheal tube, a tracheotomy, blood and fluids. An electrocardiogram monitor was attached to measure Mr. Kennedy's heart beats.

Dr. Clark was summoned and arrived in a minute or two. By then, Dr. Perry said, Mr. Kennedy was "critically ill and moribund," or near death.

Dr. Clark said that on his first sight of the President, he had concluded immediately that Mr. Kennedy could not live.

"It was apparent that the President had sustained a lethal wound," he said. "A missile had gone in and out of the back of his head causing external lacerations and loss of brain tissue."

Shortly after he arrived, Dr. Clark said, "the President lost his heart action by the electrocardiogram." A closed-chest cardiograph massage was attempted, as were other emergency resuscitation measures.

Dr. Clark said these had produced "palpable pulses" for a short time, but all were "to no avail."

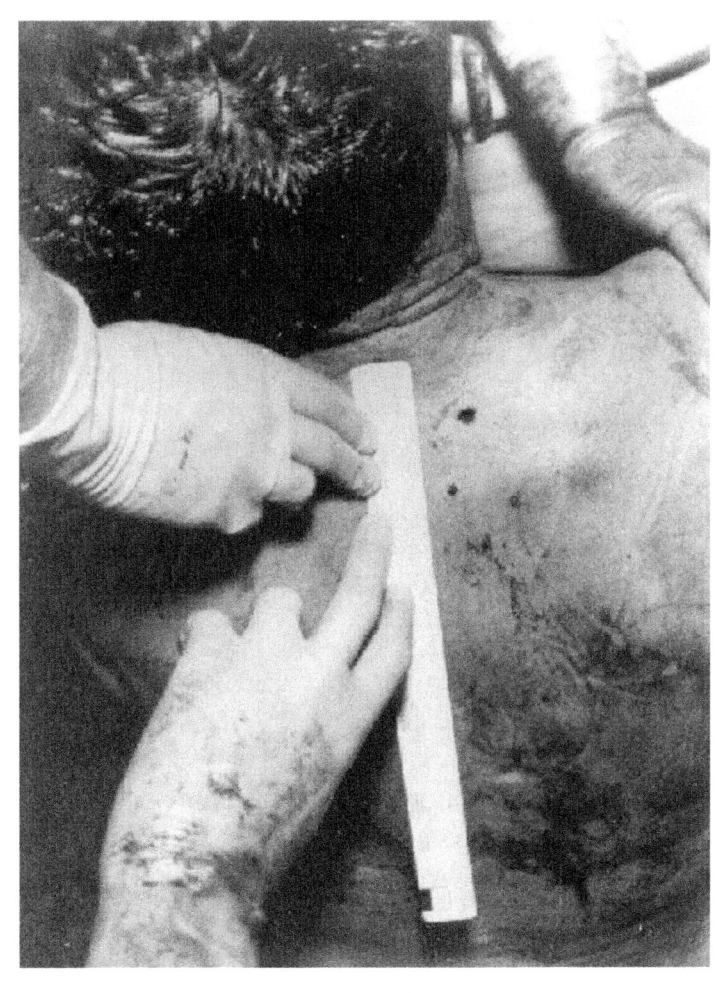

Autopsy of JFK.

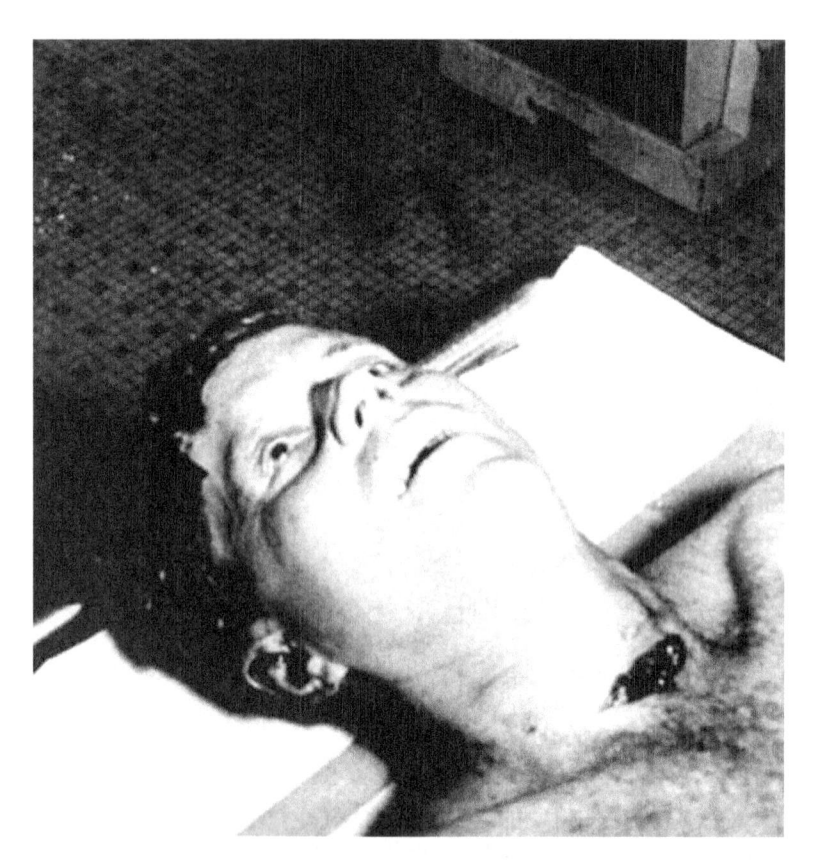

Autopsy of JFK.

Dr. Robert N. McClelland, Assistant Professor of Surgery at Parkland Hospital, responded to President Kennedy in the emergency room as he died. And, that Dr. McClelland states that the hole in the back of Kennedy's head was an exit wound, and not an entrance wound as claimed by the government (the Warren Commission). In other words, Kennedy was shot in the head from the front.

Dr. Crenshaw, who was the surgeon who worked on President Kennedy when he died. He says that he looked over Kennedy's wounds very carefully after the President was declared dead, and that Kennedy was shot twice from the front. One shot from the front went into Kennedy's head at the upper right part of his head, blowing out pieces of Kennedy's skull and brain from the back of his skull. The second wound was in the throat, just above the necktie, creating a small opening, about the size of the little finger.

Dr. Crenshaw has been a trauma surgeon for decades, and he has dealt continuously with gunshot wounds. He emphatically states that Kennedy was shot twice from the front. He also claims that someone tampered with the throat wound by significantly enlarging it (to be like a larger exit wound and not the smaller entrance wound that it was) after Kennedy was wrapped in sheets and after he helped place Kennedy into a coffin in the emergency room; and, that this wound enlargement occurred before Kennedy was photographed later, just before his autopsy at the naval hospital.

Dr. Crenshaw states that the autopsy sketches, pictures, and conclusions about Kennedy's head and neck injuries during the Kennedy autopsy, and later used by the Warren Commission as crucial evidence, do not represent Kennedy's injuries in the emergency room!

Dr. Evalea Glanges, who was outside the hospital while Kennedy was dying in the hospital, and she claims she inspected a bullet hole in the front windshield of Kennedy's limo, which she claims clearly indicated that the windshield was shot from in front of the limo.

CHAPTER THREE
THE DIRECTION OF THE SHOTS

FBI Agent Charles Taylor wrote in his report that there was a bullet hole in the front windshield of Kennedy's limo and bullet fragments were removed from it. Also, Dallas Motorcycle Police officer Stavis Ellis wrote that a pencil could be inserted through the hole in the front windshield. Dallas Patrolman Nick Prencipe recorded there was a hole in the windshield. Another witness, Harold R. Freeman, said there was a hole in the front windshield. Carl Renas, connected with the Ford Motor Company, where the Kennedy limo was re-built after the assassination, reported what appeared to be a gunshot hole in the chrome trim of the car.

Bullet hole positioned left side of the car mirror. The shot came from the left of the driver and slightly up.

First shot passes through the Presidential car window. The motorcade is heading through the triple underpass.

Kennedy is hit in the throat. The angle and height of entry places the shot coming from above the direction of the triple underpass.

Chrome hit inside window screen

The evidence of the second shot. One of the most important points of damage to the limousine was the dent of the chrome topping above the windshield. Was it caused by a direct hit of a bullet or a bullet fragment? This suggests that the second bullet meant for President Kennedy hit the chrome of the wind shield and was reflected down to Governor Connally hitting him in the back and leg. The shots according to the Chief of Police were deemed to be coming from above that would be the triple underpass that passes over Commerce, Main and Elm street. Below is the transcript of the police radio the after moments the President was shot.

Re: ASSASSINATION OF PRESIDENT
JOHN FITZGERALD KENNEDY,
NOVEMBER 22, 1963, DALLAS, TEXAS

Caller	Conversation
Dispatcher (HENSLEE)	12:30 p.m. KKB 364.
1 (Chief of Police JESSE E. CURRY)	Go to the hospital - Parkland Hospital. Have them stand by.
1 (Chief of Police JESSE E. CURRY)	Get a man on top of that triple underpass and see what happened up there.
1 (Chief of Police JESSE E. CURRY)	Have Parkland stand by.
Dallas 1 (Sheriff J. E. "BILL" DECKER)	I am sure it's going to take some time to get your man in there. Pull every one of my men in there.

Radio Transcript

Caller

Dispatcher……………………12.30 p.m.

Chief of Police………………Go to the hospital-Parkland Hospital. Have them stand by.

Chief of Police………………Get a man on top of that triple underpass and see what happened up there.

Chief of Police………………Have Parkland stand by.

Sheriff J.E. 'Bill' Decker.......I am sure it's going to take ages to get your man in there. Pull every one of my men in there.

A few minutes after President Kennedy was shot in Dealey Plaza, we see people rushing toward the "Grassy Knoll" area up towards the triple underpass. Clearly visible in this photo (on the other side of Elm Street, near the curb) are famous assassination eyewitnesses Charles Brehm and Mary Moorman.

Assessing the direction of the first, second and third shot is paramount in locating the shooter. Looking at the evidence primarily from the bullet hole found in the front car window screen © we can match that angle of impact to the location. Later in this book I give the exact place of the shooter, but let the reader fully understand, if the shot came from anywhere else other than the 5th Floor of the Texas School Depositary building then the Warren Commission conclusions are wrong i.e. Lee Harvey Oswald would be declared an innocent man.

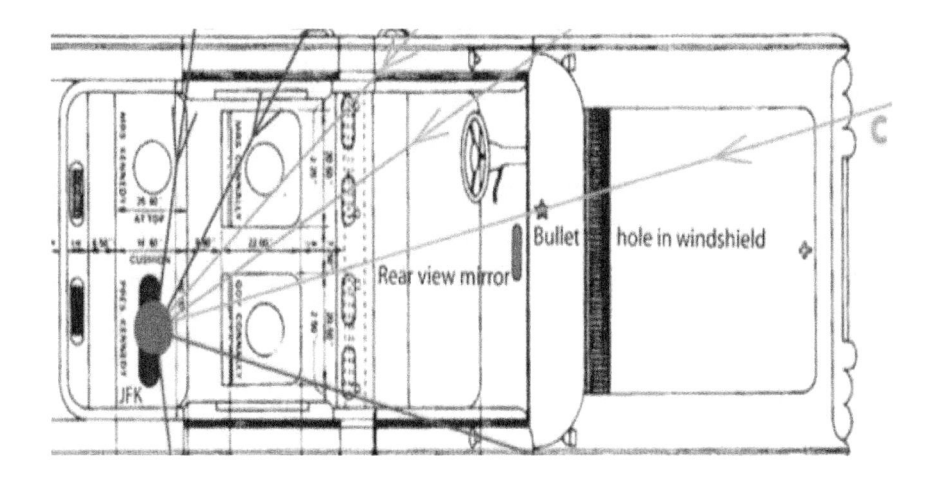

C gives the direction of shot from the front originating from the left corner of the Triple Underpass

Elm St heading towards the triple underpass. The faint x in the road marks the fatal shot. The assassin was a quality marksman practiced in hitting far away objects.

CHAPTER FOUR

ALL DIRECTIONS LEAD TO THE TRIPLE UNDERPASS

Before the Texas School Book Depositary area was flooded by Police a command was given out for everyman available to search the triple underpass. This was the first command of the Chief of Police Curry and Sheriff Decker. The Chief of Police was travelling in the first escort car in front of the Presidential motorcade. Here in the first moments of the shooting his attention was drawn to this bridge overpass. They clearly found nothing, but then it was all too late the assassin had fled the scene. But there were two Patrolmen stationed on this overpass a J. W. Foster and J.C. White. We must hear their testimonies of what they saw and heard.

Aerial view of the railroad on the Triple Underpass

TESTIMONY OF J. W. FOSTER

The Testimony of J.W. Foster was taken at 1:30 a.m., on April 9, 1964, in the office of the U.S. attorney, 301 Post Office Building, Bryan and Ervay Streets, Dallas, Tex., by Mr. Joseph A. Ball, assistant counsel of the President's Commission.

Mr. BALL - Do you solemnly swear that the testimony you are about to give before this Commission will be the truth, the whole truth, and nothing but the truth, so help you God?
Mr. FOSTER - I do.
Mr. BALL - Mr. Foster, we have requested Chief Curry to have you come in and testify in this matter before this Commission. This Commission was established to investigate the facts and circumstances surrounding the assassination of President Kennedy.
Mr. FOSTER - Yes, sir.
Mr. BALL - And my name is Joseph A. Ball. I am a staff officer, staff counsel with the Commission. I would like to ask you some questions about this matter. You are willing to testify, aren't you?
Mr. FOSTER - Yes, sir.
Mr. BALL - Will you state your address?
Mr. FOSTER - 309 Cooper Street. I just moved.
Mr. BALL - What is your occupation?
Mr. FOSTER - I am a police officer.
Mr. BALL - Dallas Police Department?
Mr. FOSTER - Yes, sir.
Mr. BALL - Patrolman?
Mr. FOSTER - Yes, sir.
Mr. BALL - How long have you been on the police department?
Mr. FOSTER - Nine years.
Mr. BALL - Where were you born and raised?
Mr. FOSTER - In Hill County, town of Hillsboro.
Mr. BALL - What was your education?
Mr. FOSTER - Well --

Mr. BALL - Where did you go to school?
Mr. FOSTER - Hillsboro.
Mr. BALL - How far through school?
Mr. FOSTER - Ninth grade.
Mr. BALL - What did you do after that?
Mr. FOSTER - Service.
Mr. BALL - What branch? Army or Navy --
Mr. FOSTER - Army.
Mr. BALL - Then what did you do?
Mr. FOSTER - Carpenter, worked for about 9 years.
Mr. BALL - Then what did you do?
Mr. FOSTER - Come to work here.
Mr. BALL - On the police department?
Mr. FOSTER - Yes.
Mr. BALL - What kind of work were you doing in November of 1963, for the Dallas Police Department?
Mr. FOSTER - I was working in the **traffic division**, investigation of accidents.

INVESTIGATOR Al Chapman (left) chats in Dealey Plaza with Dallas Police Officer J.W. Foster, who was an expert eyewitness to the assassination.

J.W. Foster. Note the white hat of the Traffic Division

Mr. BALL - Investigation of accidents?
Mr. FOSTER - Yes, sir.
Mr. BALL - Did you have a special assignment on November 22?
Mr. FOSTER - Yes, sir.
Mr. BALL - 1963. And what was that?
Mr. FOSTER - That was assigned to the triple overpass to keep all unauthorized personnel off of it.
Mr. BALL - That was the overpass, the railroad overpass?
Mr. FOSTER - Yes, sir.
Mr. BALL - Do you - the overpass runs in a north-south direction?
Mr. FOSTER - Yes, sir.
Mr. BALL - And you call it the triple overpass, why?
Mr. FOSTER - Three streets coming through there.
Mr. BALL - What are they?
Mr. FOSTER - Commerce, Main, and Elm.
Mr. BALL - I have a map that I will - just a moment. I will get it.
Mr. FOSTER - All right.
(off the record)
Mr. BALL - Tell me where you were standing on the triple overpass about the time that the President's motorcade came into sight?
Mr. FOSTER - **I was standing approximately along the - I believe the south curb of Elm Street.**
Mr. BALL - Were you on the overpass?
Mr. FOSTER - Yes, sir; at the east - be the east side of the overpass.
Mr. BALL - On the east side of the overpass?
Mr. FOSTER - Yes, sir.
Mr. BALL - Then was there another officer assigned to that same position?
Mr. FOSTER - He was assigned to the overpass with me; yes, sir.
Mr. BALL - What is his name?
Mr. FOSTER - J.C. White.

Mr. BALL - Where was he?
Mr. FOSTER - He was on the west side of the overpass.
Mr. BALL - You were on the east side?
Mr. FOSTER - Yes, sir.
Mr. BALL - Off the record.
(discussion off the record)
Mr. BALL - Let's go back on the record. Now we have a map here which we will mark as Exhibit A for your deposition.
Mr. FOSTER - Yes, sir.
Mr. BALL - And it shows the railroad overpass running in a north and south direction, is that right?
Mr. FOSTER - Yes, sir.
Mr. BALL - Over that pass comes trains into the yard, is that right?
Mr. FOSTER - Yes, sir.
Mr. BALL - And that yard is to the north and west of the Texas Book Depository Building?
Mr. FOSTER - Well, that whole thing, they have yards all over up there.
Mr. BALL - In what general direction from the Texas Scholl Book Depository Building?
Mr. FOSTER - They have yards to the north, and some to the south of it down below the Terminal.
Mr. BALL - There are yard south?
Mr. FOSTER - They have yards here[indicating].
Mr. BALL - That is north and west?
Mr. FOSTER - Yes, sir,
Mr. BALL - And also south?
Mr. FOSTER - That's right.
Mr. BALL - Now, did you see the President's motorcade come into sight?
Mr. FOSTER - Yes, sir.
Mr. BALL - Where did you see it? Where was it when you saw it?
Mr. FOSTER - When I first saw it it was coming off of Main Street onto Houston.

Mr. BALL - And did you keep it in sight?
Mr. FOSTER - Yes, sir; it was in sight most of the time.
Mr. BALL - Now where were you standing?
Mr. FOSTER - Standing along the east curb of - east side of the overpass over Elm Street there, above the south curb.
Mr. BALL - Over, above the south curb of Elm?
Mr. FOSTER - Yes, sir.
Mr. BALL - Will you put a mark on there? Mark an "X" where you were standing and write your initials right next to that "X".
J. - What are the initials?
Mr. FOSTER - J.W.
Mr. BALL - J.W.F. That marks where you were standing.
Mr. FOSTER - Approximately; yes, sir.
Mr. BALL - Did you keep the President's motorcade in sight after it turned?
Mr. FOSTER - Other than watching the men that were standing on the overpass there with me.
Mr. BALL - Now, you had instructions to keep all unauthorized personnel off of that overpass?
Mr. FOSTER - Yes, sir.
Mr. BALL - Did you do that?
Mr. FOSTER - Yes, sir.
Mr. BALL - Did you permit some people to be there?
Mr. FOSTER - Yes, sir.
Mr. BALL - Who?
Mr. FOSTER - People that were working for the railroad there.
Mr. BALL - Were there many people?
Mr. FOSTER - About 10 or 11.
Mr. BALL - Where were they standing?
Mr. FOSTER - They were standing along the east banister.
Mr. BALL - The east banister?
Mr. FOSTER - Yes, sir; in front of me.
Mr. BALL - In front of you. Will you mark there and show the general area where they were standing?
Mr. FOSTER - They were standing along this area here

[indicating].
Mr. BALL - You have marked a series of X's to show where about 10 people were standing?
Mr. FOSTER - Yes, sir.
Mr. BALL - Were you looking toward them?
Mr. FOSTER - Yes, sir.
Mr. BALL - Did you have another officer with you there on duty that day?
Mr. FOSTER - Not on that side. He was on the west side.
Mr. BALL - He was on the west side?
Mr. FOSTER - Yes, sir.
Mr. BALL - What was his name?
Mr. FOSTER - **J.C. White**.
Mr. BALL - Do you know exactly where he was when you were at the position you have indicated?
Mr. FOSTER - **No; I don't. The only thing I know, he was supposed to be on the west side of the banister.**
Mr. BALL - You were looking to the east?
Mr. FOSTER - Yes, sir.
Mr. BALL - Now, tell me what you saw happen after the President's car passed - turned onto Elm from Houston.
Mr. FOSTER - After he came onto Elm I watched the men on the track more than I was him. Then I heard this loud noise, sound like a large firecracker. Kind of dumbfounded at first and then heard the second one. I moved to the banister of the overpass to see what was happening. Then the third explosion, and they were beginning to move around. I ran after I saw what was happening.
Mr. BALL - What did you see was happening?
Mr. FOSTER - Saw the president slump over in the car, and his head looked just like it blew up.
Mr. BALL - You saw that did you?
Mr. FOSTER - Yes, sir.
Mr. BALL - And what did you do then?
Mr. FOSTER - Well, at that time I broke and ran around to my right - to the left - around to the bookstore.

Mr. BALL - Now, did you have any opinion at that time as to the source of the sounds, the direction of the sounds?
Mr. FOSTER - Yes, sir.
Mr. BALL - What?
Mr. FOSTER - It came from back in toward the corner of Elm and Houston Streets.
Mr. BALL - That was you impression at that time?
Mr. FOSTER - Yes, sir.
Mr. BALL - **Was any shot fired from the overpass?**
Mr. FOSTER - **No, sir.**
Mr. BALL - Did you see anyone with a weapon there?
Mr. FOSTER - No, sir.
Mr. BALL - Or did you here any sound that appeared to come from the overpass?
Mr. FOSTER - No, sir.
Mr. BALL - Where did you go from there?
Mr. FOSTER - Went on around the back side of the bookstore.
Mr. BALL - Immediately?
Mr. FOSTER - Yes, sir.
Mr. BALL - Did you see anybody coming out that side of the bookstore?
Mr. FOSTER - No, Sir.
Mr. BALL - Back side? What do you mean by that?
Mr. FOSTER - Well I guess you would say the northwest side of it.
Mr. BALL - Were there any people in the railroad yards around the bookstore at that time?
Mr. FOSTER - Yes, sir. There was a pretty good crowd beginning to gather back in that area.
Mr. BALL - At that time?
Mr. FOSTER - Yes, sir.
Mr. BALL - Had you seen anybody over at the railroad yard north and west of the bookstore before you heard the shots fired?
Mr. FOSTER - No; other than people that had come up there

and I sent them back down the roadway.
Mr. BALL - I see. People had attempted to get on the overpass there?
Mr. FOSTER - Yes, sir.
Mr. BALL - And you had sent them away?
Mr. FOSTER - yes, sir.
Mr. BALL - When you got over to the School Book Depository Building, what did you do?
Mr. FOSTER - I was standing around in back there to see that no one came out, and the sergeant came and got me and we were going to check the - all the railroad cars down there.
Mr. BALL - Who was that sergeant?
Mr. FOSTER - Sergeant came up there.
Mr. BALL - Did you search the railroad cars?
Mr. FOSTER - No; he sent me back down to the inspector. Told me to report back to Inspector Sawyer.
Mr. BALL - Where?
Mr. FOSTER - At the front of the book Depository.
Mr. BALL - Did you talk to Sawyer there?
Mr. FOSTER - Yes, sir.
Mr. BALL - Did you tell sergeant or Sawyer, either one where you thought the shots came from?
Mr. FOSTER - Yes, sir.
Mr. BALL - What did you then tell them?
Mr. FOSTER - Told them it came from the vicinity up around Elm and Houston.
Mr. BALL - Did you tell the sergeant that first, or did you tell that to Sawyer?
Mr. FOSTER - Told that to inspector Sawyer.
Mr. BALL - You told that to Sawyer?
Mr. FOSTER - Yes, sir.
Mr. BALL - Did you tell that to the sergeant?
Mr. FOSTER - I don't know whether I told the sergeant or not.
Mr. BALL - What did you do after that?
Mr. FOSTER - I moved to -down the roadway there, down to see if I could find where any of the shots hit.

Mr. BALL - Find anything?
Mr. FOSTER - Yes, sir. **Found where one shot had hit the turf there at the location.**
Mr. BALL - Hit the turf?
Mr. FOSTER - Yes, sir.
Mr. BALL - Did you see any marks on the street in anyplace?
Mr. FOSTER - No, **a manhole cover. It was hit.** they caught the manhole cover right on the corner and -
Mr. BALL - You saw a mark on the manhole cover did you?
Mr. FOSTER - Yes sir.
Mr. BALL - I show you a picture here of a concrete slab. or manhole cover. Do you recognize that picture?
Mr. FOSTER - Yes, sir.
Mr. BALL - Does the picture show - tell me what it shows there.
Mr. FOSTER - This looks like the corner here where it penetrated the turf right here [indicating].
Mr. BALL - See any mark on the manhole cover?
Mr. FOSTER - No, sir; I don't. not on the - well, it is on the turf, on the concrete, right in the corner.
Mr. BALL - Can you put an arrow showing the approximate place you saw that?
Mr. FOSTER - Should have been approximately along here[indicating].
Mr. BALL - Make it deep enough to mark. The arrow marks the position that you believe you saw the mark on the pavement?
Mr. FOSTER - Yes, sir.
Mr. BALL - It was not on the manhole cover?
Mr. FOSTER - No, sir.
Mr. BALL - Went into the turf?
Mr. FOSTER - Yes, sir.
Mr. BALL - Did you recover any bullet?
Mr. FOSTER - No, sir. It ricocheted on out.
Mr. BALL - Did you have the crime lab make a picture of that spot?

Mr. FOSTER - I called them to the location.
Mr. BALL - And told them to make a picture?
Mr. FOSTER - On, I didn't tell them. Called them to the spot and let them take it. Can I see the picture?
Mr. BALL - Yes, sir. Is this the picture?
Mr. FOSTER - That resembles the picture.
Mr. BALL - I offer this as "B" then. Mark it as "B" so that we have "A" and "B" now. Officer, this will be written up and submitted to you for your signature and you can read it over and change it any way you wish, or you may waive your signature at this time, which do you prefer?
Mr. FOSTER - Well, it doesn't matter.
Mr. BALL - Suit yourself. You make the choice.
Mr. FOSTER - I would just as soon go ahead and sign it.
Mr. BALL - All right. We will notify you and you can get in here and sign it.
Mr. FOSTER - All right.
Mr. BALL - Than you. One moment please. Who gave you your assignment, Mr. Foster?
Mr. FOSTER - Sergeant Harkness.
Mr. BALL - You did permit some railroad employees to remain on the overpass?
Mr. FOSTER - Yes, sir.
Mr. BALL - How did you determine they were railroad employees?
Mr. FOSTER - By identification they had with them. Identification they had and the other men that was with them verifying that they were employees.
Mr. BALL - Okay.

THE TESTIMONY OF J.C. WHITE

The testimony of J.C. White was taken at 11:45 a.m., on April 9, 1964; In the office of the U.S. attorney, 801 Post Office

Building, Bryan and Ervay Streets, Dallas, Tex., by Mr. Joseph A. Ball, assistant counsel of the President's Commission.

Award winner White, left, and Marshal Nash.

From the Dallas Morning Post 1964. J.C. White (Policeman) and Robert Irvine Nash who was present on the 23rd November at the interrogations of Lee Harvey Oswald.

Mr. BALL. All right, will you stand up and be sworn.
Do you solemnly swear that the testimony you are about to give shall be the truth, the whole truth and nothing but the truth, so help you God?
Mr. WHITE. I do.

Mr. BALL. All right.
Mr. BALL. Will you state your name, please.
Mr. WHITE. J.C. White.
Mr. BALL. What Is your residence?
Mr. WHITE. 2803 Klondite.
Mr. BALL. And your occupation?
Mr. WHITE. Policeman.
Mr. BALL. Did you receive a letter from the Commission?
Mr. WHITE. No, sir.
Mr. BALL. For a request to-
Mr. WHITE. No, sir.
Mr. BALL. You were asked to come here by your--
Mr. WHITE. Captain.
Mr. BALL. Which captain?
Mr. WHITE. Lawrence.

Mr. BALL. Now, the Commission was established to investigate the facts and circumstances surrounding the assassination of President Kennedy. We want to ask you some questions about information that you might have that might aid us In that investigation.
I am a Staff officer of the Commission named Ball. Joseph A. Ball. I am authorized to administer the oath to you, to make this inquiry. During the course of our investigation in Dallas we discovered that you and the man that you were working with that day, Mr. J. W. Foster, knew of some facts that might aid us in the investigation. We asked Chief Curry if we could have you come up here and testify, and I guess that is the reason you are here.
You are willing to testify, are you not?
Mr. WHITE. Yes, sir.
Mr. BALL. Tell us whatever you know about it.
Mr. WHITE. I don't know.
Mr. BALL. Well, I can ask you.
Mr. WHITE. Okay.

Mr. BALL. I will ask you questions. Where were you born?
Mr. WHITE. Van Alystyne, Tex.
Mr. BALL. Where did you go to school?
Mr. WHITE. Van Alystyne, Tex.
Mr. BALL. How far through school?
Mr. WHITE. Ninth grade there.
Mr. BALL. Then what did you do?
Mr. WHITE. I went into the Army.
Mr. BALL. And how long were you In the Army?
Mr. WHITE. About 3 years.
Mr. BALL. And what did you do?
Mr. WHITE. Went to driving a city bus.
Mr. BALL. How long did you drive a city bus?
Mr. WHITE. 6 years.
Mr. BALL. Then what did you do?
Mr. WHITE. Joined the Police Department.
Mr. BALL. How long ago?
Mr. WHITE. 1956.
Mr. BALL. And what are you now?
Mr. WHITE. Accident investigator.
Mr. BALL. And your rank is a patrolman?
Mr. WHITE. Yes, sir.
Mr. BALL. Now, on November22. 1963, did you have an assignment?
Mr. WHITE. Yes, sir.
Mr. BALL. Where?
Mr. WHITE. **On the triple underpass.**
Mr. BALL. And were you there with someone?
Mr. WHITE. Yes, sir.
Mr. BALL. Who?
Mr. WHITE. J. W. Foster.
Mr. BALL. Where were you?
Mr. WHITE. **Standing on the west side of the overpass.**
Mr. BALL. On the west side of the overpass?
Mr. WHITE. Yes.
Mr. BALL. Where were you with reference to Elm. Main or

Commerce as they go underneath the overpass?
Mr. WHITE. **Approximately at the north curb of Main Street.**
Mr. BALL. Approximately the north curb of Main on the corner of the north curb of Main? That would be--
Mr. WHITE. Yes, sir.
Mr. BALL. **On the west side of the overpass?**
Mr. WHITE. Yes.

Mr. BALL. I'm going to get another copy of this map. Let me see. I can use this. Mark this as Exhibit A to your deposition. Now, a diagram that was drawn by a patrolman, Joe Murphy, and he has made some marks and other witnesses have, but don't pay any attention to that. I want you to look at this drawing and take a pen and mark your position on the railroad overpass in a circle, and put your initials beside it.
You have made an "X".

Mr. WHITE. Yes, sir.
Mr. BALL. And you have initialed J.C. White, is that right?
Mr. WHITE. Yes, sir.
Mr. BALL. Over the-what would be the west curb of Main?
Mr. WHITE. North curb of Main.
Mr. BALL. The north curb?
Mr. WHITE. Yes.
Mr. BALL. North curb of Main?
Mr. WHITE. Yes, sir.
Mr. BALL. And west side of the overpass?
Mr. WHITE. Yes, sir.

Mr. BALL. Is there a rail there?
Mr. WHITE. Yes, sir.
Mr. BALL. How many people were on that overpass that day?
Mr. WHITE. On the same side I was on?

Mr. BALL. Yes.
Mr. WHITE. None.
Mr. BALL. None? Any people attempt to come up on the overpass around noon?

Standing positions on the triple underpass of Foster and White at the time of the shooting. Foster was on the east side and White on the Westside.

Mr. WHITE. Not on my side.
Mr. BALL. They did not?
Mr. WHITE. No, sir.
Mr. BALL. Had you seen your partner send any people away from the overpass?
Mr. WHITE. Yes, sir.
Mr. BALL. You had certain instructions, didn't you?
Mr. WHITE. Yes, sir.
Mr. BALL. What were they?
Mr. WHITE. Not to let any unauthorized personnel on top of the overpass.

Mr. BALL. Now, you did permit some people to stay on the overpass, didn't you?
Mr. WHITE. Yes, sir.
Mr. BALL. Who were they?
Mr. WHITE. Workers of the railroad company.
Mr. BALL. Were they people you knew?
Mr. WHITE. No, sir.
Mr. BALL. Well, how did you know they were workers with the railroad company?
Mr. WHITE. Majority of them were there when we got there, working on the rails.
Mr. BALL. And you let them stay there?
Mr. WHITE. Yes, sir.
Mr. BALL. **Did you see the President's car come into sight?**
Mr. WHITE. **No, sir; first time I saw it it has passed, passed under the triple underpass.**
Mr. BALL. You were too far away to see it, were you?
Mr. WHITE. **There was a freight train traveling. There was a train passing between the location I was standing and the area from which the procession was traveling, and-a big long freight train, and I did not see it.**
Mr. BALL. You didn't see the procession?
Mr. WHITE. No, sir.
Mr. BALL. Before the train went by, did you see some railroad personnel over on the-would it be the--
Mr. WHITE. East side?
Mr. BALL. East side of the overpass?
Mr. WHITE. Yes, sir.
Mr. BALL. How many people?
Mr. WHITE. About 10, approximately. I didn't count them.
Mr. BALL. Did you hear any shots?
Mr. WHITE. No, sir.
Mr. BALL. Didn't?
Mr. WHITE. No, sir.
Mr. BALL. **First time you saw the President's car it was**

going underneath?

Mr. WHITE. **Yes, sir**.

Mr. BALL. What did you do after that?

Mr. WHITE. **As soon as the train passed I went over and on the northwest side of the Depository Building.** On the northwest side of the book store up there with the rest of the officers and after about 30 minutes they told me to go out and work traffic at Main and Houston, and I stood out there and worked traffic.

Mr. BALL. All right, now, you heard no sound of no rifle fire or anything?

Mr. WHITE. No, sir.

Mr. BALL. **Freight train was going through at the time?**

Mr. WHITE. **Yes, sir.**

Mr. BALL. Making noise?

Mr. WHITE. Yes, sir; noisy train.

Mr. BALL. Mr. White, Mr. Foster was on the east side of the overpass?

Mr. WHITE. Yes, sir.

Mr. BALL. This deposition will be written up and submitted to you for your signature if you wish to sign it, or you can waive your signature. Which do you wish to do?

Mr. WHITE. You said a while ago to him it would be written up like this? Is that correct?

Mr. BALL. No, It will be written up in the form of a deposition.

Mr. WHITE. I will waive.

Mr. BALL. You waive it. Okay. Fine.

A photo taken after the shooting the presidential car has just passed under the triple underpass on the way to Parkland hospital.

The photo MAGNIFIED shows that there was not a freight-train passing at the time of the shooting as stated in the testimony of White and there is no sight of White on this

Westside of Main on the triple underpass where he stated he was standing.

TESTIMONY OF EARLE V. BROWN

The testimony of Earle V. Brown was taken at 4:40 p.m., on April 7, 1964. in the office of the U.S. attorney, 801 Post Office Building, Bryan and Ervay Street, Dallas, Tex., by Messrs. Joseph A. Ball and Samuel A. Stern, assistant counsel of the President's Commission

Mr. BALL Would you please rise, raise your right hand and be sworn?
Mr. BROWN. All right.
Mr. BALL. Do you solemnly swear the testimony you will give will be the truth, the whole truth, and nothing but the truth, so help you God?
Mr. BROWN. I do.
Mr. BALL. Sit down, State your name and address, please..
Mr. BROWN. Earle V. Brown, 618 North Rosemont.
Mr. BALL. What is your occupation?
Mr. BROWN. Policeman.
Mr. BALL. With the Dallas Police Department?
Mr. BROWN. Yes, sir.
Mr. BALL How long have you been a policeman?
Mr. BROWN. Fourteen years.
Mr. BALL. Where were you born and what is your education and training?
Mr. BROWN. I was born on a farm near Lyons, Nebraska, in 1917, and I completed 12 years of schooling, high school.
Mr. BALL. High school?
Mr. BROWN. Yes, sir.
Mr. BALL. Then what did you do?
Mr. BROWN. Well, I stayed on the farm until 1939, then I moved to Ohio; Lima, Ohio. I was inducted into the Army and was in there 4 years, 5 months, discharged 1945, August 15,

and I was here in Dallas actually when I was discharged and then back to Ohio for about 4 years. Then, let's see, that would be August of 1949, we came back to Dallas and then February 27, 1950, I joined the police force.
Mr. BALL. Now, you are a patrolman, aren't you?
Mr. BROWN. Yes, sir.
Mr. BALL. On November , 1964, were you assigned to a certain post on duty?
Mr. BROWN. Yes, sir.
Mr. BALL. Where?
Mr. BROWN. That would be the railroad overpass over Stemmons Expressway service road.

The location of the Stemmons Freeway railroad overpass

Mr. BALL. Is that the one that leads of Elm?
Mr. BROWN. You mean that crosses Elm?
Mr. BALL. That crosses Elm, yes; the overpass across Elm.
Mr. BROWN. No, sir.

Mr. BALL. What does it cross?
Mr. BROWN. It's over Stemmons Expressway; in other words, they make that turn of Elm and go up.
Mr. BALL. You know where Elm, the corner of Elm and Houston is?
Mr. BROWN. Yes, sir.
Mr. BALL. Then there Is a road, the highway continues on to the west, a little south, is that what you call the Stemmons Expressway?
Mr. BROWN. There's one there, too, but that overpass is actually a road. Where I was was the railroad overpass.
Mr. BALL. The railroad overpass Itself?
Mr. BROWN. Yes, sir.
Mr. BALL. How far were you from the place where the continuation of Elm goes under the overpass?
Mr. BROWN. Oh, approximately 100 yards.
Mr. BALL. Let me see if we can get something In the record that will be your position. You were appointed to this particular spot?
Mr. BROWN. Yes, sir.
Mr. BALL. Was there another patrolman on the overpass also?
Mr. BROWN. Yes, sir; James Lomax.
Mr. BALL. Now, this Is the place where the railroad yards run over the highway?
Mr. BROWN. Yes.
Mr. BALL. And you are on the **Stemmons Freeway** end of It?
Mr. BROWN. That's right; In other words, Stemmons Freeway and the service road both go under the underpass.
Mr. BALL. What is his name?
Mr. BROWN. James Lomax.
Mr. BALL. How far were you from the point where Elm Street goes under the underpass?
Mr. BROWN. I would say approximately 100 yards.
Mr. BALL. approximately 100 yards in what direction?
Mr. BROWN. That would be - wouldn't be straight east, but It

would be to easterly, kind of off at an angle - I would say about from us about a 20 degree angle to the right.
Mr. BALL. You would be east or west?
Mr. BROWN. We would be to the southwest of that.
Mr. BALL. You would be to the southwest of that?
Mr. BROWN. Yes, I would say that's about right.
Mr. BALL. Did you have the corner of Houston and Elm Street in sight from where you were located?
Mr. BROWN. Actually, we could see cars moving there, you know, coming and making the turn, but the intersection, that would be about all we probably could see would be cars.
Mr. BALL. Could you see cars going down after they made the turn and going down toward the underpass south?
Mr. BROWN. Yes.
Mr. BALL. You could see those?
Mr. BROWN. Yes.
Mr. BALL. Did you have any instructions when you were assigned to this location?
Mr. BROWN. Yes, sir.
Mr. BALL. What were they?
Mr. BROWN. Not allow anyone on the overpass whatever and walk forward and make both ends-in other words, check both ends of the overpass.
Mr. BALL. That was you and Mr. Lomax?
Mr. BROWN. That's right.
Mr. BALL. Was there an E. V. Brown?
Mr. BALL. That's me.
Mr. BALL. That's you, and was there also a Joe Murphy?
Mr. BROWN. Joe Murphy is a three-wheeler.
Mr. BALL. Yes; where was he?
Mr. BROWN. I don't know, sir; he was, I believe he was on his three-wheeler.
Mr. BALL. On his motor?
Mr. BROWN. I believe; I wouldn't say for sure but I don't know.
Mr. BALL. Did you people keep people off the overpass?
Mr. BROWN. We made no contact with anyone except one of

the railroad detectives come up there and talked to us.
Mr. BALL. Did you keep the underpass free of people?
Mr. BROWN. Underneath?
Mr. BALL. No; up above.
Mr. BROWN. Up above; yes, sir.
Mr. BALL. What about underneath?
Mr. BROWN. Well, that was roadway there; people wouldn't be able to walk
Mr. BALL. On the top of the overpass you kept that free of people?
Mr. BROWN. Yes, sir.
Mr. BALL. Did you have the railroad yards In sight?
Mr. BROWN. Yes, sir.
Mr. BALL. They would he what direction from where you were standing?
Mr. BROWN. That would he east; that would he east of us.
Mr. BALL. East, maybe a little north?
Mr. BROWN. Yes, the whole thing kind of in that general direction, you know.
Mr. BALL. Did you see any people over In the railroad yards?
Mr. BROWN. Not that I recall; now they were moving trains in and out.
Mr. BALL. But you did not see people standing?
Mr. BROWN. No, sir; sure didn't.
Mr. BALL. Everything was in clear view?
Mr. BROWN. Yes, sir.
Mr. BALL. I withdraw the question. Was there any obstruction of your vision to the railroad yards?
Mr. BROWN. Yes.
Mr. BALL. What?
Mr. BROWN. Not the direction of the railroad yard, but at ground level we didn't have very good view. Mr. Lomax and I remarked that we didn't have a very good view.
Mr. BALL. **Was that because of the moving trains?**
Mr. BROWN. **Yes, sir.**
Mr. BALL. Did you see the President's motorcade come on to

Houston Street from Elm; were you able to see that?
Mr. BROWN. Now they came down Main, didn't they, to Houston?
Mr. BALL. Yes.
Mr. BROWN. No. sir; actually, the first I noticed the car was when it stopped.
Mr. BALL. Where?
Mr. BROWN. After it made the turn and when the shots were fired, it stopped.
Mr. BALL. Did It come to a. complete stop?
Mr. BROWN. That, I couldn't swear to.
Mr. BALL. It appeared to be slowed down some?
Mr. BROWN. Yes; slowed down.
Mr. BALL. Did you hear the shots?
Mr. BROWN. Yes, sir.
Mr. BALL. How many?
Mr. BROWN. Three.
Mr. BALL. Where did they seem to come from?
Mr. BROWN. Well, they seemed high to me, actually; if you want, would you like me to tell you?
Mr. BALL. Sure, tell it in your own words.
Mr. BROWN. Well, down in that river bottom there, there's a whole lot of pigeons this particular day, and they heard the shots before we did because I saw them flying up - must have been 50, 75 of them.
Mr. BALL. Where was the river bottom?
Mr. BROWN. You know, actually off to the - between us and the, this over pass you are talking about there's kind of a levee along there. It's really a grade of the railroad, is what it is; that's where they were and then I heard these shots and then I smelled this gun powder.
Mr. BALL. You did?
Mr. BROWN. It come on it would be maybe a couple minutes later so - at least it smelled like It to me.
Mr. BALL. What direction did the sound seem to come from?
Mr. BROWN. It came it seemed the direction of that building,

that Texas ---
Mr. BALL. School Book Depository?
Mr. BROWN. School Book Depository.
Mr. BALL. Did you see any pigeons flying around the building?
Mr. BROWN. I Just don't recall that; no, sir.
Mr. BALL. Which way did you look when you heard the sound?
Mr. BROWN. When I first heard that sound I looked up toward that building because actually it seemed to come from there.
Mr. BALL. Where was it you saw the pigeons rise?
Mr. BROWN. They must have been down there feeding at that time because they just seemed to all take off.
Mr. BALL. Where were they from where you were standing?
Mr. BROWN. From where I was standing they would be about half way between - no, they would be up more toward that other overpass, whet they call the triple underpass.
Mr. BALL. **The triple underpass?**
Mr. BROWN. Yea.
Mr. BALL. You were about 100 yards from the triple underpass?
Mr. BROWN. Approximately; yes.
Mr. BALL. Was there anybody standing on the triple underpass?
Mr. BROWN. On the triple underpass?
Mr. BALL. Yes.
Mr. BROWN. **Yes, sir; they had at least two officers.**
Mr. BALL. Anybody but police officers?
Mr. BROWN. Not that I know of. I didn't recall anyone.
Mr. BALL. What did you do after you heard the shots?
Mr. BROWN. Well, let me see, by that time the escort as to the motorcycles, we could see them coming, the front part of the motorcade, I don't think they probably realized what happened; they had come on ahead. And then we saw the car coming with the President, and as it passed underneath me I looked right down and I could see this officer in the back; he had this gun and he was swinging it around, looked like a

machinegun, and the President was all sprawled out, his foot on the back cushion. Of course, you couldn't conceive anything that happened; of course, we knew something had happened, but we couldn't conceive the fact it did.

Mr. BALL Did you move out of there in any direction?

Mr. BROWN. No, sir; we, well, we checked there; the area, we kept checking that area through there and, of course, there were people all over the place but we didn't allow anybody up on the railroad right-of-way through there.

Mr. BALL. Was there anybody standing on the triple underpass at the point where Elm goes underneath?

Mr. BROWN. Uh-uh, I couldn't recall; no one except police officers.

Mr. BALL. More than one?

Mr. BROWN. Yes.

Mr. BALL. Did you search any part of the area?

Mr. BROWN. We were instructed to stay at our posts, which we did, and later we got instructions to check the area around the Depository, Book Depository Building, and to obtain the license numbers of all those cars parked around there, which we did.

Mr. BALL. Where were any cars parked?

Mr. BROWN. Well, there's a parking lot around that building and there was several cars parked all around that building.

Mr. BALL. You took the license numbers?

Mr. BROWN. Yes; in fact, I think there must have been four or five officers taking license numbers.

Mr. BALL. How long were you around there?

Mr. BROWN. Well, we stayed and then they sent us back to the overpass and we stayed there until, let's see, I don't believe we left there until about 3:30 or 4 In the afternoon, and then we came up to the hall and Mr. Sorrels, I believe talked to us.

Mr. BALL. I think that's all, officer. This will be written up and you can take it, read it, and sign it if you wish, or you can waive your signature, just as you wish. Which do you wish?

Mr. BROWN. You mean today?
Mr. BALL. No; it will be a week or so.
Mr. BROWN. Oh, yes.
Mr. BALL. Which do you prefer?
Mr. BROWN. What preference do I have?
Mr. BALL. Well, It will be written up and you can come in and sign it --
Mr. BROWN. Yes.
Mr. BALL. Or you can waive signature and you don't need to come In and sign It. It is your option; you can do either way.
Mr. BROWN. I will be glad to come in and sign it.
Mr. BALL. She will notify you. Thanks very much.

TESTIMONY OF EARLE V. BROWN RESUMED

The testimony of Earle V. Brown was taken at 2:15 p.m., on April 8, 1964, In the office of the U.S. attorney, 301 Post Office Building, Bryan and Ervay Streets. Dallas, Tex., by Mr. Joseph A. Ball. assistant counsel of the President's Commission.

Mr. BALL You have been sworn, so we will just continue with your deposition, and your name is Earle V. Brown?
Mr. BROWN. Right; E-a-r-l-e (spelling).
Mr. BALL. Mr. Brown, I have had a map made here which I would like to have you inspect here. The railroad overpass is shown - that runs in a north and south direction?
Mr. BROWN. Yes.
Mr. BALL. And Stemmons Freeway overpass is shown - that runs north and south, doesn't it?
Mr. BROWN. Right.
Mr. BALL. Were you on either one of those overpasses?
Mr. BROWN. Either one of those two there?
Mr. BALL. Yes.
Mr. BROWN. No, sir.
Mr. BALL. Where were you?
Mr. BROWN. On this overpass here - this TP Railroad

overpass.

Mr. BALL. The overpass that runs in an east and west direction?

Mr. BROWN. Right - yes, sir.

Mr. BALL. Now, will you take this pen and draw on there your position on the overpass?

Mr. BROWN. Well, you see, on this overpass, of course, there are the tracks and then there is a railing and then there is a catwalk on each side and we walked the catwalk, and we would come around on each end and we would walk the tracks and come around there.

Mr. BALL. Where were you when you saw the President's car turn on Houston and Elm Street?

Mr. BROWN. I was on the catwalk.

Mr. BALL. Can you mark your position?

Mr. BROWN. I would be - approximately in the center.

(Instrument marked by the witness, as requested by Counsel Ball.)

Mr. BALL. Have you marked the place where you were?

Mr. BROWN. Yes; It would be about the center of that.

Mr. BALL. Is that where you were when you heard the shots?

Mr. BROWN. Yes.

Mr. BALL And did you see anybody out on the railroad overpass?

Mr. BROWN. No, sir; I didn't see anybody there.

Mr. BALL. You don't recall seeing anybody that would either be where Elm goes under the overpass or where Main goes under the overpass - you don't recall seeing anybody?

Mr. BROWN. No; I don't recall seeing anyone there.

Mr. BALL. You told me yesterday you saw some officers.

Mr. BROWN. Well, that would be the police officers - would be the only ones I saw.

Mr. BALL. **Do you know who those officers were?**

Mr. BROWN. **No, sir; at the time I did, but I wouldn't know now.**

Mr. BALL. Did you see any officer on Stemmons Freeway where we have positioned (1), (2),and (3) on this diagram?
Mr. BROWN. No, I didn't.
Mr. BALL. Now, the place where you marked your location - we will mark that as Brown Exhibits - the X marks the position of Brown, Is that correct?
Mr. BROWN. Yes.
Mr. BALL. That's all Thank you very much.
Mr. BROWN. All right.
(Instrument marked by the reporter as "Brown Exhibit A," for Identification.)
Mr. BALL. Thank you very much for coming.
Mr. BROWN. All right.

Three statements and we find Foster where he says he was on the east side of the triple underpass. We have photo evidence to prove that his statement is true (I shall provide the photographic evidence later). But the testimony of White appears to be odd. He was the only man that day amongst hundreds of witnesses that heard no shots, even Brown on Stemmons Freeway a hundred yards back from the triple underpass heard the shots clearly. Also, it is a fact the Police Department stopped all trains that day from passing on the triple underpass while the motorcade was passing through.
Yet White states a very long freight train passed on the triple underpass the moment the President JFK was assassinated.
Interestingly Foster never sighted White that day, it is almost as if White indeed was not there, but somewhere else. Was his place momentarily replaced by another for P.O. Brown saw two Policeman but could not remember who they were.

CHAPTER FIVE

THE WITNESSES

John Dolan and James Tague

James Tague was the third man wounded during the JFK assassination in Dallas on November 22, 1963. He was standing on Commerce Street under the triple underpass when he was slightly wounded in the face by debris from a missed shot that hit the Main Street curb. Tague, who died in February 2014, became a respected JFK researcher and authored two books on the assassination. But his story about what happened right after the shooting underwent an intriguing change after his Warren Commission testimony.

" So I stood there (at the bridge abutment) looking around. . . and about that time a patrolman who evidently had been stationed under the triple underpass walked up and said, 'What happened?' and I said, 'I don't know; something.'" Tague went on to testify that "we" (he and this patrolman) walked over to the area of the grassy knoll where a crowd was gathering, and a few minutes later, we walked back down there, and another man joined us who identified himself as the deputy sheriff, who was in civilian clothes." This was Buddy Walthers, who tells Tague "you have blood there on your cheek."

That was Tague's first account of what happened, clearly placing him in the company of a uniformed police officer ("a patrolman"), with the two of them joined minutes later by a deputy sheriff in civilian clothes. Yet this "patrolman" who was "evidently stationed under the triple underpass" who asked Tague "What happened?" would simply disappear from all of Tague's accounts after his WC testimony, leaving only the deputy sheriff in Tague's company.

According to the Warren Commission's final report, forensic tests by the FBI revealed that the chipped bullet mark impact location contained no embedded copper metal residue, indicating that it was not created by "an unmutilated military full metal-jacketed bullet such as the bullet from Governor Connally's stretcher."

A selection of witnesses of what they heard and seen.

DEPUTY SHERIFF EUGENE BOONE -- "Well, it was approximately 1 o'clock when we heard the shots. The motorcade had already passed by us and turned back to the north on Houston Street. And we heard what we thought to be a shot. And there seemed to be a pause between the first shot and the second shot and third shots--a little longer pause. And we raced across the street there."

DEPUTY SHERIFF JACK FAULKNER (via the Sheriff's Report filed by Faulkner on 11/22/63) -- "I was standing on the corner of Main and Houston, when the presidential motorcade came by. A few seconds later I heard three shots and the crowd began to move enmasse toward Elm Street."

DEPUTY SHERIFF C.M. JONES (via the Sheriff's Report filed by Jones on 11/22/63) -- "Friday Morning, November the 22nd, 1963, between the hours of approximately 12 noon and 12:35pm, I was standing in front of the Criminal Courts Building talking with Allan Sweatt and Robert Benevides and awaiting the arrival of the motorcade bearing the President's party. The motorcade passed in front of us and everything appeared to be in order. A few short seconds later I heard an explosion, followed in about 3 to 5 seconds later two more explosions. I am certain that I recognized the second two as being that of gunfire."

DEPUTY SHERIFF W.W. MABRA (via the Sheriff's Report filed by Mabra on 11/27/63) -- "I and officer Orville Smith were standing on the curb in front of [the] Criminal Courts Building, approximately 40 feet east of Houston St., when the car bearing President Kennedy passed. Approximately 1 minute after the car turned right onto Houston St., we heard 3 shots."

DEPUTY SHERIFF A.D. McCURLEY (via the Sheriff's Report filed by McCurley on 11/22/63) -- "I was standing at the front entrance of the Dallas Sheriff's Office at 505 Main Street, Dallas, as the President's motorcade passed and was watching the remainder of the parade pass when I heard a retort [sic; report] and I immediately recognized it as the sound of a rifle. I started running around the corner where I knew the President's car should be, and in a matter of a few seconds heard a second shot and then a third shot."

DEPUTY SHERIFF LUKE MOONEY (via the Sheriff's Report filed by Mooney on 11/23/63) -- "I was standing in front of the Sheriff's office at 505 Main Street, Dallas, when President Kennedy and the motorcade passed by. Within a few seconds after he had passed me and the motorcade had turned the corner, I heard a shot, and I immediately started running towards the front of the motorcade, and within seconds heard a second and a third shot."

DEPUTY SHERIFF CHARLES P. PLAYER (via the Sheriff's Report filed by Player on 11/22/63) -- "Mr. Decker, I watched the motorcade pass on Record St. from your office window. After the President's car passed I started back to my desk. I heard three shots and went back to the window. People were running in all directions. I left the office by the back door and went across the street to where my squad car was parked on the side street just back of the book depository."

SHERIFF'S OFFICER L.C. SMITH (via the Sheriff's Report filed by Smith on 11/22/63) -- "Just shortly before 12:30pm, Friday, November 22, 1963, I was standing in front of the Sheriff's Office on Main Street and watched the President and his party drive by. Just a few seconds later, I heard the first shot, which I thought was a backfire, then the second shot and third shot rang out. I knew then that this was gun shots and everyone else did also."

DEPUTY SHERIFF ALLAN SWEATT (via the Sheriff's Report filed by Sweatt on 11/23/63) -- "At approximately 12:30 PM, Friday, November 22, 1963, I was standing with a group of Deputy Sheriffs about 30 feat [sic] east of the corner of Houston and Main Street on Main Street. The president's caravan had just passed and about a minute or 2 I heard a shot, and about 7 seconds later another shot and approximately 2 or 3 seconds later a third shot, which sounded to me like a rifle and coming from the vicinity of Elm and Houston Street."

DEPUTY SHERIFF L.C. TODD (via the Sheriff's Report filed by Todd on 11/27/63) -- "On November the 22nd, 1963, I had come on duty at 9am working the information window at the Dallas County Jail. About 12:15pm, the window was closed where I worked and I walked outside and onto Houston Street to view the President's motorcade as it passed. A few seconds after the President's car passed me and had turned the corner of Houston onto Elm Street, I heard what I first thought was a backfire. I heard a total of 3 and after the last two (2), I immediately recognized them as being gun fire."

DEPUTY SHERIFF RALPH WALTERS (via the Sheriff's Report filed by Walters on 11/23/63) -- "I was standing on Main Street in front of the Criminal Courts Building the morning of November 22, 1963, and observed the Presidential procession pass by. Just after it had turned the corner and a very short time later, I heard what was [sic] shots, 3 in number."

DEPUTY SHERIFF EDDY "BUDDY" WALTHERS (via the Sheriff's Report filed by Walthers on 11/22/63) -- "I was standing at the front entrance of the Dallas Sheriff's Office when the motorcade with President Kennedy passed. I was watching the remainder of the President's party when within a few seconds I heard a retort [sic; report], and I immediately recognized it to be a rifle shot. I immediately started running west across Houston Street and ran across Elm Street and up into the railroad yards. At this time it was not determined if, in fact, this first retort [sic] and 2 succeeding retorts [sic] were of a rifle. However, in my own mind, I knew."

SHERIFF'S OFFICER "RADIO" WATSON (via the Sheriff's Report filed by Watson on 11/22/63) -- "I had just looked out the window of the radio room facing Main Street and watched the Presidential parade pass and as it turned the corner onto Record [Street], I looked over in that direction but was unable to see any of the vehicles from my location and about that time I heard three loud reports, evenly spaced, which I presumed to be rifle or shotgun blast. I looked at the time on the radio panel and it was about 40 seconds after 12:30pm as I was calling Dallas PD on the hot line, and I asked the operator that answered if anything had been reported, and she said no. I told her that I heard what I believed to be three shots, and she thought I was kidding."

CHAPTER SIX

A VISION TO THE SLAUGHTER

The triple underpass is made up of three road carriages, from left to right, Commerce, Main and Elm. The Presidential limousine was travelling in the middle lane of Elm Street when JFK was assassinated, taking three bullets. The first photos of the shooting are massively important. Here we see Officer Foster over Elm St, his testimony given to WC is true.

Potter (avant plan) et Foster

This picture is of the east side of Elm St. and shows patrolman Fosters position over the triple underpass at the time of the shooting. Note: He wears a white hat. **We also see the rail road workers on the triple underpass.**

President Trump recently presided over the releasing of the JFK files, whose most significant information is given below.

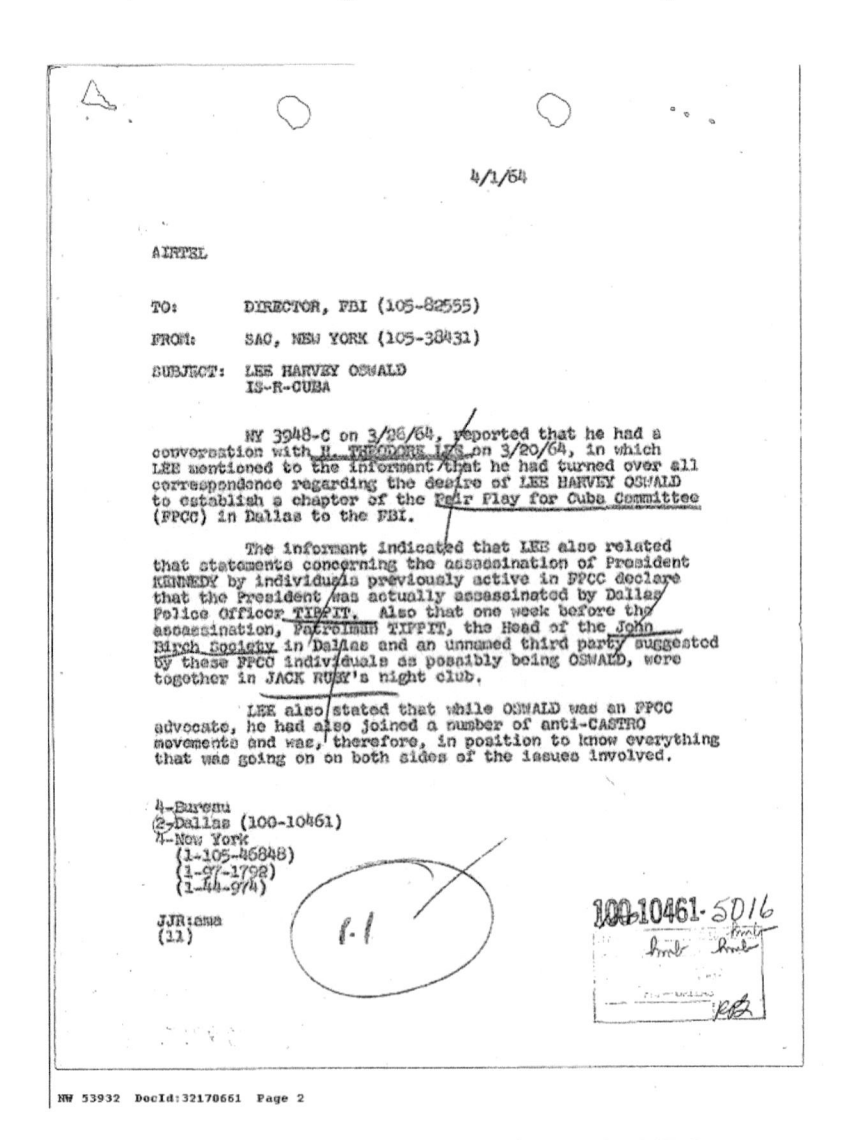

4/1/64

AIRTEL

TO: DIRECTOR, FBI (105-82555)
FROM: SAC, NEW YORK (105-38431)
SUBJECT: LEE HARVEY OSWALD
IS-R-CUBA

NY 3948-C on 3/26/64, reported that he had a conversation with H. THEODORE IVES on 3/20/64, in which LEE mentioned to the informant that he had turned over all correspondence regarding the desire of LEE HARVEY OSWALD to establish a chapter of the Fair Play for Cuba Committee (FPCC) in Dallas to the FBI.

The informant indicated that LEE also related that statements concerning the assassination of President KENNEDY by individuals previously active in FPCC declare that the President was actually assassinated by Dallas Police Officer TIPPIT. Also that one week before the assassination, Patrolman TIPPIT, the Head of the John Birch Society in Dallas and an unnamed third party suggested by these FPCC individuals as possibly being OSWALD, were together in JACK RUBY's night club.

LEE also stated that while OSWALD was an FPCC advocate, he had also joined a number of anti-CASTRO movements and was, therefore, in position to know everything that was going on on both sides of the issues involved.

4-Bureau
2-Dallas (100-10461)
4-New York
  (1-105-46848)
  (1-97-1792)
  (1-44-974)

JJR:ama
(11)

100-10461-5016

NW 53932 DocId:32170661 Page 2

The note from the newly released JKF files.

According to the note sent to the FBI, an informant was told by an H. Theodore Lee in that 'the president was actually assassinated by Dallas police officer TIPPIT'.

```
that the President was actually assassinated by Dallas
Police Officer TIPPIT. Also that one week before the
assassination, Patrolman TIPPIT, the Head of the John
Birch Society in Dallas and an unnamed third party suggest
by these FPCC individuals as possibly being OSWALD, were
together in JACK RUBY's night club.
```

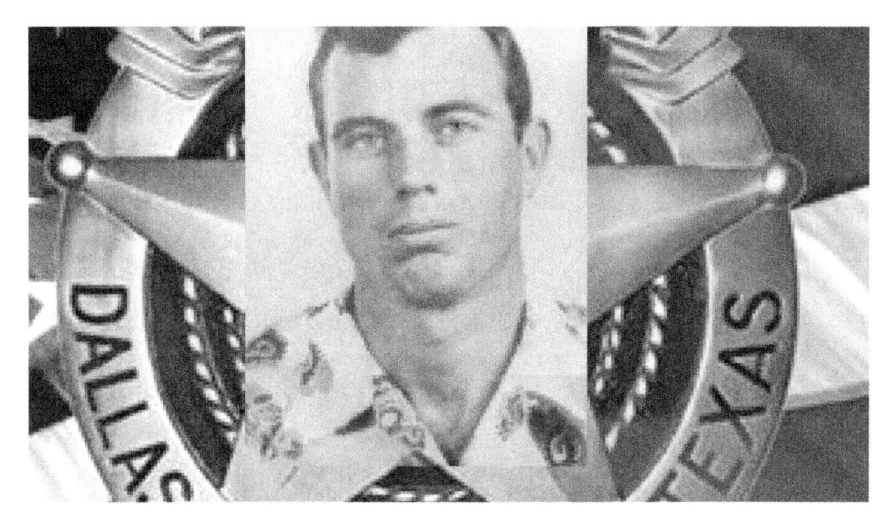

J.D. Tippit who meet his death shortly after JFK

The note also says a week before the assassination Tippit, allegedly head of the right-wing John Birch Society in Dallas, and a third party who was possibly Oswald, met in Jack Ruby's nightclub.

It is supposed that the informant was referring to J.D. Tippit above but according to Jack Ruby he never knew J. D. Tippit but did know a G. M. Tippit in the Dallas Police Department.

Extract of the Testimony of Mr. Jack Ruby

Early Friday afternoon, Nov. 22, Ruby remarked how he knew Tippit, the officer who had been shot by Oswald. Later Ruby stated that he did not know J.D. Tippit but that his reference was to G.M. Tippit, a member of the special services bureau of the Dallas Police Department who had visited Ruby establishments during the course of his official duties."

The President's Commission met at 11:45 a.m., on June 7, 1964, in the interrogation room of the Dallas County Jail, Main and Houston Streets, Dallas, Tex. Present were Chief Justice Earl Warren, Chairman; and Representative Gerald R. Ford, member. Also present were J. Lee Rankin, general counsel; Joseph A. Ball, assistant counsel; Arlen Specter, assistant counsel; Leon Jaworski and Robert G. Storey, special counsel to the attorney general of Texas; Jim Bowie, assistant district attorney; Joe H. Tonahill, attorney for Jack Ruby; Elmer W. Moore, special agent, U.S. Secret Service; and J. E. Decker, sheriff of Dallas County.

Mr. RANKIN. Did you know Officer Tippit?
Mr. RUBY. I knew there was three Tippits on the force. The only one I knew used to work for the **special services**, and I am certain this wasn't the Tippit, this wasn't the man.
Mr. RANKIN. The man that was murdered. There was a story that you were seen sitting in your Carousel Club with Mr. Weissman, Officer Tippit, and another who has been called a rich oil man, at one time shortly before the assassination. Can you tell us anything about that?
Mr. RUBY. Who was the rich oil man?
Mr. RANKIN. Can you remember? We haven't been told. We

are just trying to find out anything that you know about him.

Mr. RUBY. I am the one that made such a big issue of Bernard Weissman's ad. Maybe you do things to cover up, if you are capable of doing it.

As a matter of fact, Saturday afternoon we went over to the Turf Bar lounge, and it was a whole hullabaloo, and I showed the pictures "Impeach Earl Warren" to Bellocchio, and he saw the pictures and got very emotional.

And Bellocchio said, "Why did the newspaper take this ad of Weissman?"

And Bellocchio said, "I have got to leave Dallas."

And suddenly after making that statement, I realized it is his incapability, and suddenly you do things impulsively, and suddenly you realize if you love the city, you stay here and you make the best of it. And there were witnesses.

I said, "The city was good enough for you all before this. Now you feel that way about it." And that was Bellocchio.

As far as Tippit, it is not Tippitts, it is not Tippitts it is Tippit.

Mr. RANKIN. This Weissman and the rich oil man, did you ever have a conversation with them?

Mr. RUBY. There was only a few. Bill Rudman from the YMCA, and I haven't seen him in years.

And there is a Bill Howard, but he is not a rich oil man. He owns the Stork Club now. He used to dabble in oil.

Chief Justice WARREN. This story was given by a lawyer by the name of Mark Lane, who is representing Mrs. Marguerite Oswald, the mother of Lee Harvey Oswald, and it was in the paper, so we subpenaed him, and he testified that someone had given him information to the effect that a week or two before President Kennedy was assassinated, that in your Carousel Club you and Weissman and Tippit, Officer Tippit, the one who was killed, and a rich oil man had an interview or conversation for an hour or two.

Dallas Police Officer G.M. "Tip" Tippit, a Lake Highlands resident, was off duty on Nov. 22, 1963. He knew Jack Ruby well and frequented his club.

THE OBITUARY OF G.M. TIPPIT

Gayle Marshall "Tip" Tippit, Badge No. 710, served the Dallas department for 30 years, including work as a detective. He was not related to Officer Jefferson Davis "J.D." Tippit, who was killed by Lee Harvey Oswald on Nov. 22, 1963. But he did know Jack Ruby, who killed Oswald on live television.

G.M Tippit, 96, died Tuesday at Texas Health Presbyterian Hospital Dallas of complications after a fall Nov. 16. 2015.

"He never talked a lot about his police work," said his son, Jerry Tippit of Quinlan. "He did enjoy it, I do know that."

Tippit was an outgoing and friendly man who enjoyed hunting and fishing, his son said.

"He liked to be out at the deer lease on opening day," his son said.

Tippit was born in Cleburne on Christmas Day 1919. He grew up in Sherman and Royse City, where he graduated from high school.

He worked for the Brown Shipbuilding Co. in Houston, helping to make the type of landing craft he would later serve on when he joined the Navy in 1944.

He served aboard a USS LSM 312, a Landing Ship Medium that delivered supplies during amphibious landings on Pacific islands.

During one island landing, Japanese soldiers were positioned on a mountain with twin peaks. The enemy position made it hard for the Americans to return fire through the glare of the rising morning sun, Tippit told his son.

"That's probably the only story he really told me about it," Jerry Tippit said of his father's war experience.

After the war, Tippit worked in Houston and Dallas. He joined the Dallas police force in 1950, becoming a patrolman in 1951.

"I think it was something he always wanted to do," his son said.

Tippit became a detective in 1956 and was promoted to sergeant in 1968.

Not long after Tippit began working as a patrolman, he met Jack Ruby, who was operating the Silver Spur, a dance and beer tavern on South Ervay Street.

Tippit was assigned to the Special Service Bureau, which investigated narcotics and vice. He continued to occasionally check on Ruby, who became a downtown club operator.

"The Carousel Club was one of the stops on his beat," Jerry Tippit said, referring to another of Ruby's clubs. "He and Jack Ruby knew each other fairly well."

Tippit told investigators he didn't know of Oswald before the assassination and had no information linking Ruby and the assassin.

Tippit was with the Dallas police helicopter unit when he retired, his son said.

A 32nd-degree Scottish Rite Mason, Tippit was a member of East Dallas Masonic Lodge 1200.

From the Dallas News

THE FREEMASON CONNECTION

The Masons Symbol

To me, G. M. Tippit appears to be the most likely suspect in the killing of JFK, and it is too my consternation that the facts of the assassination point to him as being the likely assassin. He had the perfect disguise, he was a Police Officer, and he had the opportunity, for he was off-duty at the time, and his testimony that he was working alone in his garage cannot be accounted for. But for me the most important clue that points to him as an assassin, is his affiliation to the Masonic lodge. He was a Master Mason, and Freemasons in the early 60's were under attack by Catholics notably, President Kennedy. His one story he left his son is symbolic of Freemasonry, I shall recount it below:

'During one island landing, Japanese soldiers were positioned on a **mountain with twin peaks**. The enemy position made it hard for the Americans to return fire through the glare of **the rising morning sun**. Tippit told his son.'

 Now we know the mind of the assassin, we can reconstruct the conspiracy in accordance with the symbol of the Masons.

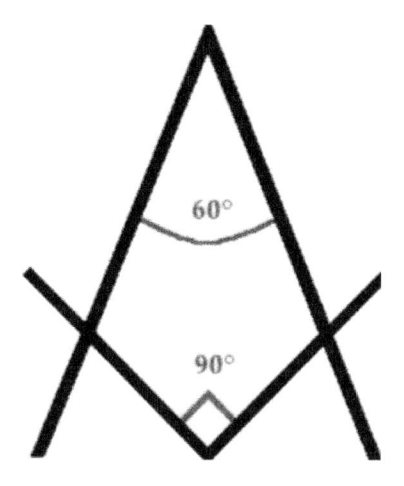

Now within this symbol there are two, degree angles.

The How of the Assassination

For the final shot location, we use the 60-degree angle. It provides us with the locations for the shooting positions. The angle shows that one assassin is on the triple underpass above Commerce St the second, behind the stockade fence.

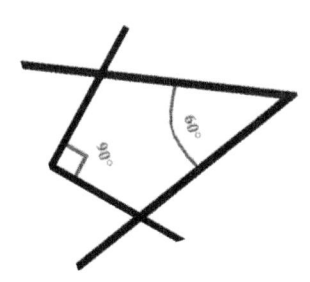

The Mason 60-degree angle

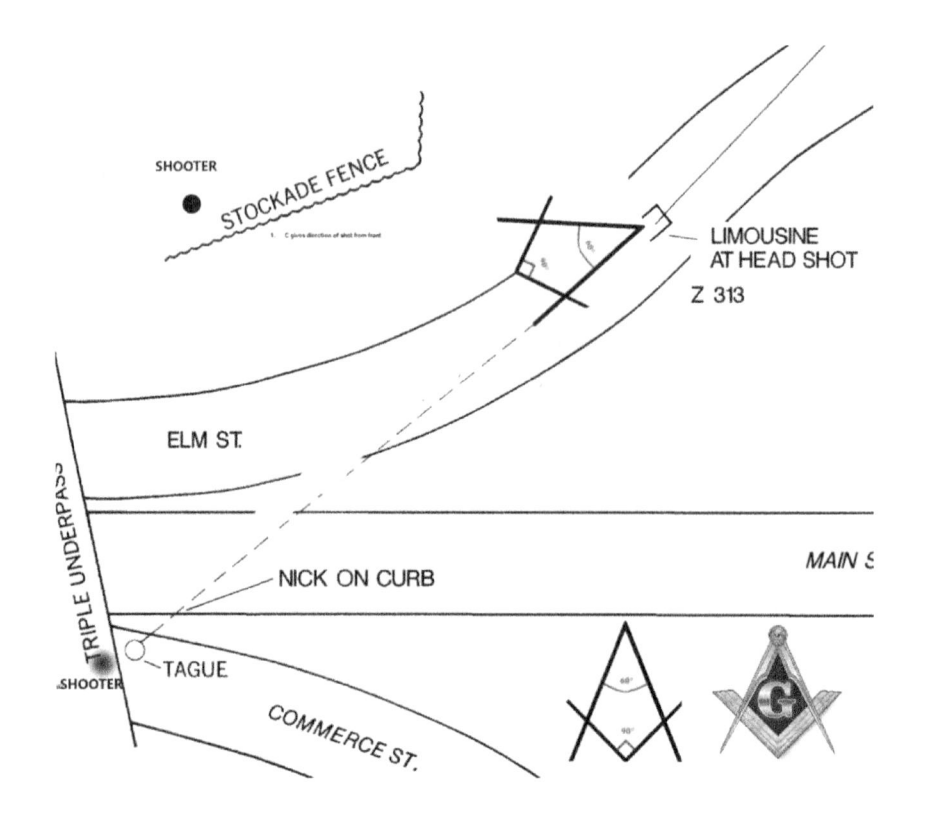

Below is a very important photo, that I have scrutinised very carefully. These are the moments after the assassination the picture tells its own story it reveals the people on the triple underpass at that moment. All my calculations of the trajectory of the first bullet places it as coming from this area. This photographic evidence gives us the scene on Elm St, Main St and just a partial bit of Commerce St. It's the only photo of its kind that details this amount of area of the triple underpass moments, seconds even after the assassination.

The chaotic scene on Elm Street immediately after JFK was shot. This photo depicts some of the "camera cars" that were part of the Dallas motorcade. A reporter makes a wild dash toward the middle car, as the driver hits the brakes to allow him to catch up. Also visible on the left side of this picture, standing near the Triple Underpass bridge, is eyewitness James Tague, who was slightly injured on the cheek during the shooting.

Witness James Tague can be seen on the corner of Main St east side of the triple underpass in the left corner.

But look at the top far-left corner

Take a closer look at the figure laying at ground level on the triple underpass

This dark figure is a Dallas Policeman laying at ground level looking between the 3rd and 4th pillars on the east side of the triple underpass positioned over Commerce St exactly moments after the shooting. He should not be there. Note: **Flat topped" hats are worn by officers riding in cars, and by Inspectors and above. Traffic (like highway patrol) officers wear white hats for visibility.** This figure is not wearing the white hat of the Traffic Division so, this Policeman is neither, Foster or White.

Foster and White according to the Warren Commission were the only Patrol Officers on the Triple Underpass at the time of the shooting of President Kennedy. No other Patrol Officer according to the Warren Commission was on the triple underpass apart from Foster and White.

The likely position of the second shooter the Stockade fence on the 'Grassy Knoll.'
Photo by Mary Moorman

THE JACK THE RIPPER CASE

NOTE FROM AUTHOR

The Whitechapel murders were a public scandal and remain a historical mystery. Anyone looking into the case is drawn to its unsolvable nature. There are as many Ripperologist's as there are names put forward as the, would be, 'Yours Truly, Jack the Ripper.' A name he gave himself. This book is unlike any other, it is unique. I do not draw the reader into a conspiracy, a dead end, but deal with the facts. I do not waste the reader's imagination, but draw them into a simple conclusion based on research. The reader of course is wary, for if there really is a solution to the murders they would have been solved at the time in the nineteenth century. This time lapse will necessarily hinder anyone solving the crimes, but we do have historical documents and real witnesses. I do not make any apology for my conclusions. Justice belongs to the victims, not to the chief of priests a system they have made. In this small volume we shall uncover the man behind the mask of 'Jack the Ripper, 'who for a century has eluded us in London's fog. The reader I leave to make up their own mind.

London 2017

BACKGROUND

Dorset St

We are drawn to the scene of the east end in the later-half of the nineteenth century a squalid area of depravity, where life existed on the breadline, when a strong drink became a man's or a woman's alleviation against this adversity of a hell on earth. Where women became prostitutes, for a mere coin that bought a drink, a bed for the night or a scrap of food. Morality, temperance and those upright values the Christian Church hold dear was least on the minds of the starving the desperate the forgotten. Domestic quarrels, murders, violence, drunkenness, bodies battered, cut and stabbed, and bruised, was just a daily occurrence for people in the East End of London. But one man's actions changed that insensitivity to all that depravity. He literally ripped and gauged the organs of his victims with a most vicious brutally.

The canonical five 'Jack the Ripper' victims are Mary Ann 'Polly' Nichols, Annie Chapman, Elizabeth Stride, Catherine Eddowes and Mary Jane Kelly.

There were many other victims of violence, but these bear the trade mark of the serial killer the maniac of Whitechapel. A clever man, with a saucy sense of humour, a light-hearted friend he called himself. He knew the streets of the east end like the back of his hand, every hidden doorway. Every nook and cranny, every alley, every back yard, he knew them as his domain.

His tyranny began in the year 1888, a number significant like the year 999AD when Christendom believed the return of Christ was imminent, or the year 1999, when the world feared the computer systems would come to a sudden halt bringing chaos and financial turmoil. The numerology system gives 888 as the number given to the Christian Messiah. In Christian numerology, the number 888 represents Jesus, or sometimes more specifically Christ the Redeemer. This representation may be justified either through gematria, by counting the letter values of the Greek transliteration of Jesus' name, or as an opposing value to 666, the number of the beast. The number becomes a quadruple number 8 for on the 31st August he met his first victim Mary Ann Nichols.

31st August being the 8th month in the year 1888 thus we have 8888 and if we divide 8888 by 31 we get the year 286AD. A period is known as the Sixth Primitive Persecution.

CHAPTER ONE

THE LADIES

Mary Ann 'Polly' Nichols

Mary Ann 'Polly' Nichols was born, 26th August in 1845 in Shoe lane. She was the daughter of a blacksmith, Edward Walker, who survived her to at her inquest. Not more than 5ft she had delicate features with grey eyes. Mary married in 1864 and had five children. Am up and down marriage she finally separated from her husband William Nichols in 1881. She left him to bring up, the children on his own, possibly because of his unfaithfulness. Even so he was required to pay her support payments, but won his claim to stop payment when he evidently proved that she was living with another man. Women had few alternatives to employment. They were essentially left to their own devices. In the East End that often meant prostitution. In the words for life, for her so apt, she was

full of grace, she was born a Tuesday's child. Mentally very quick, and a great communicator she would have been fastidiously clean in nature. Being a Virgo her relationships were to her everything, never to be abused.
It was her husband's affair with the nurse that took care of her that dealt the last blow to their relationship. She left him moving from work house to work house, then she finally found employment as a domestic servant.

Polly writes to her father:

"I just right to say you will be glad to know that I am settled in my new place, and going all right up to now. My people went out yesterday and have not returned, so I am left in charge. It is a grand place inside, with trees and gardens back and front. All has been newly done up. They are teetotalers and religious so I ought to get on. They are very nice people, and I have not too much to do. I hope you are all right and the boy has work. So good bye for the present.

from yours truly,

Polly

Answer soon, please, and let me know how you are."

After two months work, she left her employment stealing three pounds and ten shillings. Back in the workhouse she then finds lodgings at 18 Thrawl Street, Spitalfields. On the 30th August Polly spends all the money she has in the Frying Pan Pub, returning to her lodgings, she is turned away for not having the doss money for a bed for the night. Worse for wear through drink she takes solace in her new bonnet to gain the business for her doss money, too solicits for trade.

At 3.40am Polly is discovered murdered down Buck's Row.

Annie and John Chapman

Annie Chapman aka, Dark Annie was born September, 1841 in East London. She was the daughter of a soldier, George Smith. Who at the time of his death was listed a servant. Not more than five feet tall, she had dark wavy hair, stout in build and had lovely blue eyes. She suffered from tuberculosis. Annie married in 1869 to a John Chapman a coachman, by trade. After having three children the couple separated by mutual consent in 1884. Until his death her husband paid for her support. This stopped in 1886 he died on Christmas day. She was living with John Sivvey, who left her as soon as her husband died, when the money stopped coming. She moved to a lodging house in Dorset Street. She met Edward Stanley a bricklayer who paid for her lodgings. He also at the time was keeping a second woman, it was due to this a fight broke out between her and Annie. Annie gets a black eye as a result. She returns to the lodging house and while eating a baked potato, she is asked to pay doss money. John Evans the night watchman tells her:

"You can find money for your beer and you can't find money for your bed."

Annie'a parting words:

"I won't be long, Brummy. See that Tim keeps the bed for me."

Annie then sets out to do the business to get the money for a bed. On the morning of 8th September at 6.00am Annie is discovered murdered in the back yard of 29, Hanbury Street.

Annie's Clothes and Possessions:

Long black figured coat that came down to her knees.

Black skirt, Brown bodice, another bodice, 2 petticoats

A large pocket worn under the skirt and tied about the waist with strings (empty when found)

Lace up boots

Red and white striped woolen stockings

Neckerchief, white with a wide red border

Had three recently acquired brass rings on her middle finger (missing after the murder)

Scrap of muslin, one small tooth comb, one comb in a paper case

Scrap of envelope she had taken from the mantelpiece of the kitchen containing two pills. It bears the seal of the Sussex Regiment. It is postal stamped "London,

28,Aug., 1888" inscribed is a partial address consisting of the letter M, the number 2 as if the beginning of an address and an S

Elizabeth Stride

Elizabeth Stride aka, 'Long Liz' was born November 27th, 1843 north of Gothenburg, Sweden. She enters London in 1866, in the service of a foreign gentleman. She is single. In 1869 she marries John Stride and lives at 67 Gower Street.
There she moves to Poplar where with her husband she keeps a coffee shop. All things being well until her husband dies, so she claimed (no record exists) in a sea tragedy in 1878. Yet records show he actually died in 1884. Elizabeth

was an intelligent girl, she was bi-lingual she could speak Jewish. In the words for life, for her so apt, she was fair of face, she was born a Monday's child. Quite and generous by nature, a freedom lover, she often rebels against any form of restrictions. In 1885 Elizabeth Stride is living with a young partner Michael Kidney, but leaves him for periods to go off on the town. On the evening of her death she was seen with a man outside Brick Layers Arms public house. Later she was seen with another man in Berner Street and then with a man in Fairclough Street. At 1am she was found dead in Dutfield's Yard.

At the time of her death Elizabeth Stride was wearing:

Long black cloth jacket, fur trimmed around the bottom with a red rose and white maiden hair fern pinned to it.

Black skirt, Black crepe bonnet

Checked neck scarf knotted on left side

Dark brown velveteen bodice, 2 light serge petticoats

1 white chemise, white stockings, spring sided boots

2 handkerchiefs (one, the larger, is noticed at the post-mortem to have fruit stains on it.)

A thimble, a piece of wool wound around a card

In the pocket in her underskirt:,

A key (as of a padlock), A small piece of lead pencil

Six large and one small button, a comb

A broken piece of comb, a metal spoon

A hook, a piece of muslin

One or two small pieces of paper

She is found clutching a packet of Cachous in her hand. Cachous is a pill used by smokers to sweeten their breath.

Catherine Eddowes

Catherine Eddowes aka, Kate Kelly she was born April 14th, 1842, in Graisley Green, Wolverhampton. Her father was a tin plate worker. A little above five foot in height, she had hazel eyes with dark auburn hair. She suffered from Uremia.
By nature, she liked to take the lead, an organizer, and had a strong empathy for material things, and who felt most at home in a material environment. In the words for life, for her so apt, she has far to go, she was born a Thursday's child. There is

no evidence she married but she had three children through Thomas Conway. They lived on his pension and from books sold. In 1881 they split, Catherine taking the girl. She moved to Cooney's lodging house in Dean Street and met John Kelly. He worked on the market stalls. She was described as 'not often in drink, a jolly woman, often singing.'

But she had money troubles, and she was seen pawning her shoes, and was, to visit her daughter in Bermondsey to lend money. But she never arrived she was found intoxicated on the pavement arrested and sent to Bishopshgate Station. At 12.55am sober, she was released from her cell and appears to head toward Aldgate high street. At 1.35am she is seen at the corner of Duke Street and Church Passage with a man. At 1.45am PC Watkins discovers her body in Mitre Square.

Wearing at the time of her murder:

Black straw bonnet trimmed in green and black velvet with black beads. Black strings, worn tied to the head.

Black cloth jacket trimmed around the collar and cuffs with imitation fur and around the pockets in black silk braid and fur. Large metal buttons.

Dark green chintz skirt, 3 flounces, brown button on waistband. The skirt is patterned with Michaelmas daisies and golden lilies.

Man's white vest, matching buttons down front.

Brown linsey bodice, black velvet collar with brown buttons down front

Grey stuff petticoat with white waistband

Very old green alpaca skirt (worn as undergarment)

Very old ragged blue skirt with red flounces, light twill lining (worn as undergarment)

White calico chemise. No drawers or stays

Pair of men's lace up boots, mohair laces. Right boot repaired with red thread

1 piece of red gauze silk worn as a neckerchief

1 large white pocket handkerchief

1 large white cotton handkerchief with red and white bird's eye border

2 unbleached calico pockets, tape strings

1 blue stripe bed ticking pocket

Brown ribbed knee stockings, darned at the feet with white cotton

Possessions

2 small blue bags made of bed ticking

2 short black clay pipes, 1 tin box containing tea

1 tin box containing sugar, 1 tin matchbox, empty

12 pieces white rag, some slightly bloodstained

1 piece coarse linen, white, 1 piece of blue and white shirting, 3 cornered

1 piece red flannel with pins and needles

6 pieces soap, 1 small tooth comb

1 white handle table knife, 1 metal teaspoon

1 red leather cigarette case with white metal fittings

1 ball hemp, 1 piece of old white apron with repair

Several buttons and a thimble

Mustard tin containing two pawn tickets, One in the name of Emily Birrell, 52 White's Row, dated August

31, 9d for a man's flannel shirt. The other is in the name of Jane Kelly of 6 Dorset Street and dated September 28, 2S for a pair of men's boots. Both addresses are false.

Printed handbill and according to a press report- a printed card for 'Frank Carter, 305, Bethnal Green Road

Portion of a pair of spectacles

1 red mitten

Mary Kelly

Mary Jane Kelly, aka, Mary Ann Kelly, fair Kelly was born 1863 she was the youngest vctim of the Ripper being just 25 years old when she was murdered. We have no birth date, but we can tell by her photo that she was charismatic, had charm. She was five foot seven inches tall, blond hair with a fair complexion and was of Irish decent. She was born in Limerick. As a child she moved with her family to Wales, she was said to be able to speak Welsh. She arrived in London in 1884. It is claimed she went to work in a high class brothel in the West End. In 1886 she lives at 'Cooley's Lodging house and meets Joseph Barnett an Irishman. Later they both move to 13 Miller's Court off Dorset Street. After an argument her partner goes to live at Buller's boarding house. The reason is not clear but it is claimed by Barnett, that Mary was allowing prostitutes to use the small room at Miller's court. She herself was also an active participate. A witness saw her with a man heading down, Miller' Court. At 10.45 am her body is found in her room, mutilated beyond recognition.

CHAPTER TWO

THE MURDERS

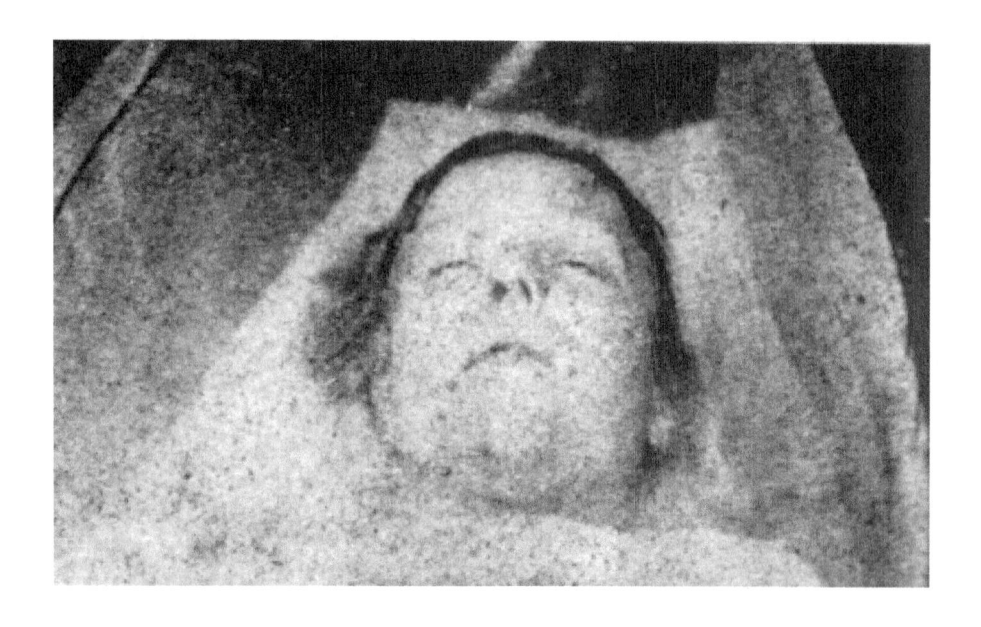

Mary Nichols (26th Aug 1845 – 31st Aug 1888)

Mary Nichols' body was discovered at about 3:40 a.m. on Friday 31 August 1888 in Buck's Row (now Durward Street), Whitechapel. The throat was severed by two cuts, and the lower part of the abdomen was partly ripped open by a deep, jagged wound. Several other incisions on the abdomen were caused by the same knife.

The location in Buck's Row of Mary Nichol's body

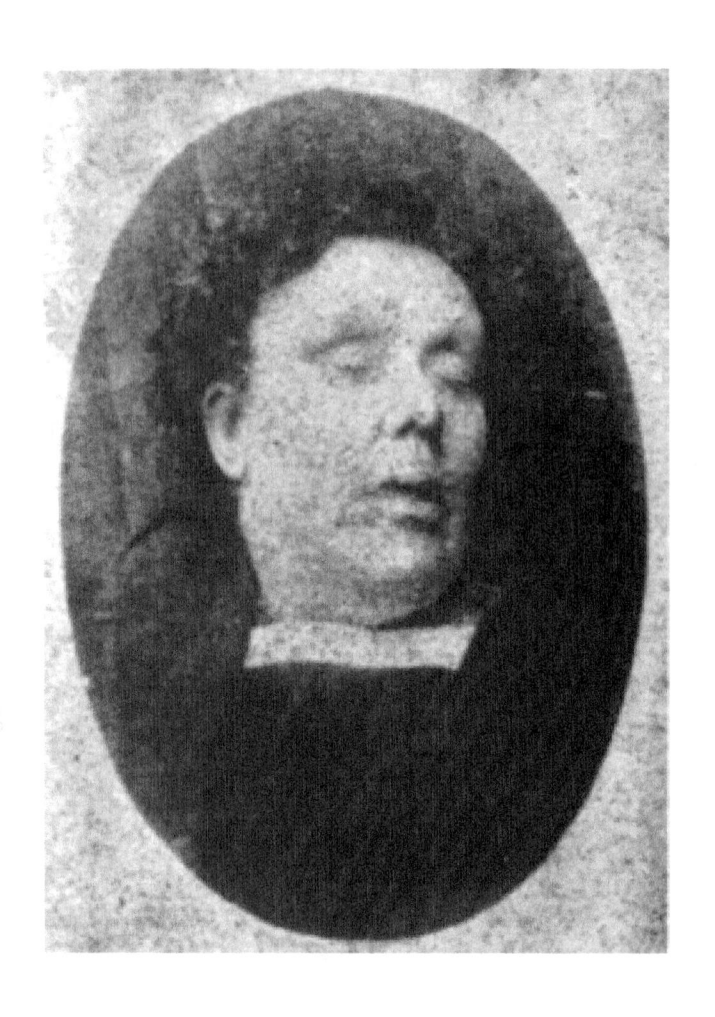

Annie Chapman (Sept 1841- 8th Sept 1888)

Annie Chapman's body was discovered at 6:00 a.m. on Saturday 8 September 1888 near a doorway in the back yard of 29 Hanbury Street, Spitalfields. As in the case of Mary Ann Nichols, the throat was severed by two cuts. The abdomen was slashed entirely open, and it was later discovered that the uterus had been removed. At the inquest, one witness described seeing Chapman at about 5:30 a.m. with a dark-haired man of "shabby-genteel" appearance.

The location of Annie Chapman's body 29 Hanbury St.

Elizabeth Stride (27th Nov 1843 - 30th Sept 1888)

Elizabeth Stride's body was discovered at about 1 a.m. on Sunday 30 September 1888 in Dutfield's Yard, off Berner Street (now Henriques Street) in Whitechapel. The cause of death was one clear-cut incision which severed the main artery on the left side of the neck. The absence of mutilations to the abdomen has led to uncertainty about whether Stride's murder should be attributed to the Ripper or whether he was interrupted during the attack. Witnesses thought that they saw Stride with a man earlier that night but gave differing descriptions: some said that her companion was fair, others dark; some said that he was shabbily dressed, others well-dressed

The location of Elizabeth Stride's body at Dutfield'Yard off Berner Street

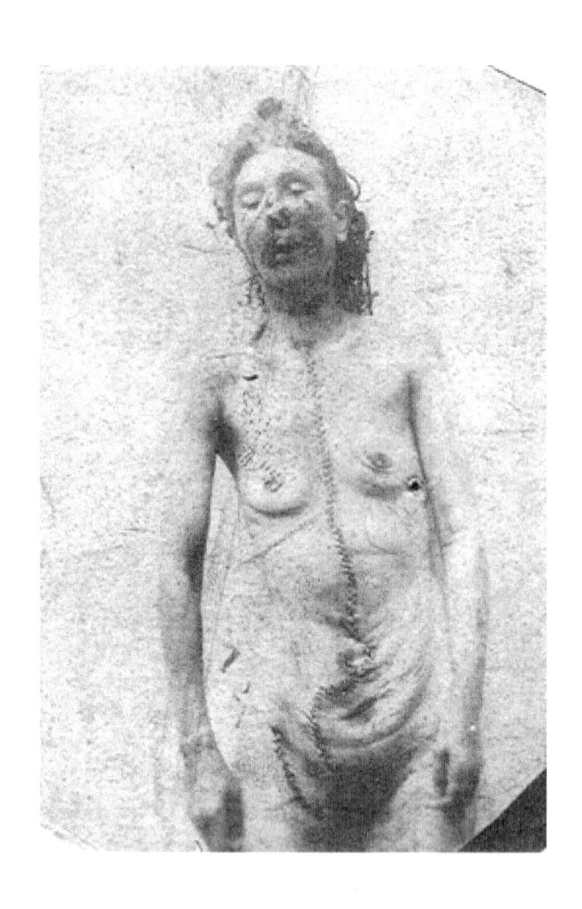

Catherine Eddowes (April 14th 1842 – 30th Sept 1888)

Catherine Eddowes' body was found in Mitre Square in the City of London, three-quarters of an hour after Stride's. The throat was severed and the abdomen was ripped open by a long, deep, jagged wound. The left kidney and the major part of the uterus had been removed. A local man named Joseph Lawende had passed through the square with two friends shortly before the murder, and he described seeing a fair-haired man of shabby appearance with a woman who may have been Eddowes. His companions were unable to confirm his description. Eddowes' and Stride's murders were later called the "double event" Part of Eddowes' bloodied apron was found at the entrance to a tenement in Goulston

Street, Whitechapel. Some writing on the wall above the apron piece became known as the Goulston Street graffito and seemed to implicate a Jew or Jews, but it was unclear whether the graffito was written by the murderer as he dropped the apron piece, or was merely incidental. Such graffiti were commonplace in Whitechapel. Police Commissioner Charles Warren feared that the graffito might spark anti-semitic riots and ordered it washed away before dawn.

Mitre Square the location of Catherine Eddowes body

Writing on the wall

On September 30, 1888, after the Ripper killed Elizabeth Stride and Catherine Eddowes, he walked northeast from Mitre Square to Goulston Street and wrote in a piece of white chalk on the black fascia of the doorway to the Wentworth Model Dwellings. Beneath a bloodied portion of apron from Eddowes clothing was found. This shows the tracks of the Ripper heading east for he was heading back home after the murders. It is the only clues he left the Police.

> "The Juwes are
> The Men that
> Will not
> be Blamed
> for nothing."

The writing - with its double negative and written in a rounded, `schoolboy,' hand.

The Ripper is clearly anti semitic, he is trying to implicate the Jews, for the murders. Also the emphasis on Men, as if from a woman's or a boy's point of view. This writing on the wall was removed by the police commissioner General Sir Charles Warren for fear that it might stir up a riot, so he said. But even so he destroyed crucial evidence. This note is mysterious and unique in several ways. What has interested researchers is the misspelling of 'Juwes' the U having supplanted the E since it should read 'Jews. Clearly it is a puzzle to solve and I believe that Sir Charles Warren knew the answer. He would of known that the U refers to the Jewish head tefilla where is written the Hebrew letter U. Notice its four club like symbol, Elizabeth Stride was the fourth victim of Jack the serial killer.

The Head Tefilla are small boxes used on the head
in prayer with the Hebrew Letter U inscribed

Mary Kelly (1863 - 9th Nov 1888)

Mary Kelly's mutilated and disembowelled body was discovered lying on the bed in the single room where she lived at 13 Miller's Court, off Dorset Street, Spitalfields, at 10:45 a.m. on Friday 9 November 1888. The throat had been severed down to the spine, and the abdomen almost emptied of its organs. The heart was missing.

The location of Mary Kelly's body 13 Miller's court

CHAPTER THREE

THE WITNESSES

Mary Ann 'Polly' Nichols

August 31st, 1888; Whitechapel, London

Ellen Holland, who was Mary's roommate at the Willmott's Lodging House, was out late that evening.

She came across Mary on the corner of Osborn Street and Whitechapel Road at 2:30 am. Mary was drunkenly leaning against a wall, and bragged that she'd made her doss money three times over, but had already drunk it away.

"I've had my doss money three times today and spent it. It won't be long before I'm back."

Ellen tried to convince her to come back to the lodging house, but Mary refused. She was set on earning the money back one more time, claiming she would simply find a man to share a bed with after one more attempt. Ellen watched Mary wobble her way back down East Whitechapel Road.

It would be the last time anyone would see her alive.

At 3:40am on the morning of August 31st, a carter named Charles Cross made his way down Buck's Row on his way to work. In the early morning darkness, Cross stopped at the sight of a large object lying in the doorway of a horse stable. He walked closer to investigate, thinking it was a tarpaulin abandoned in the street. A few feet closer, though, he realized the figure on the ground was human. As he hesitated, unsure of how to proceed, he heard another man's approaching footsteps.

It was another carter, Robert Paul, also headed to work. Cross called the other carter over, telling him that there was a woman in the street. Together, in the dark, the two men approached the figure stretched out on the ground. She was lying prone, her skirts pulled up to her waist. Tentatively, they felt her hands and face, finding them cold. Cross thought that he sensed some movement in her chest, though, which allowed the possibility that she was alive. The men tugged her skirts down over her knees to at least cover her up, and argued whether they should prop her up in the doorway.

They were unsettled by the whole incident though, and they were both running late for work. They decided not to render further assistance on the scene, justifying their behavior by agreeing to tell the first constable they ran into on their way about what they had seen. They left the woman's body alone on Buck's Row, lying across the gateway. Minutes later they came across PC Mizen 55H.

Mary Nichols body found

"She looks to me to be either dead or drunk," Cross said to the constable, "but for my part I think she is dead."

If either of the men had possessed a lantern, however, there would have been no question that Polly Nichols was dead.

Llewelyn's surviving notes taken by Spratling upon an initial examination of the body summarize findings this way:

...her throat had been cut from left to right, two distinct cuts being on left side, the windpipe, gullet and spinal cord being cut through; a bruise apparently of a thumb being on the right lower jaw, also one on left cheek; the abdomen had been cut open from centre of bottom of ribs along right side, under pelvis to left of the stomach, there the wound was jagged; the omentum, or coating of the stomach, was also cut in several places, and two small stabs on private parts; [all] apparently

done with a strong bladed knife; supposed to have been done by some left handed person; death being almost instantaneous.

Annie Chapman

September 8th, 1888; Hanbury Street, Spitalfields

As the nearby brewery clock struck 5:30, Mrs. Durrell, was walking along Hanbury Street when she passed a man and a woman standing against No. 29. The man's back was to her so she couldn't see his face, but he was dressed in a long black coat and was wearing, a deerstalker hat.

As she passed, she heard the man say, **"Will you?"**

The woman, whom shelater identified as Annie Chapman, replied, **"Yes."**

At 5:15 am, a young carpenter who lived at No. 27 Hanbury Street named Albert Cadosch went out into his backyard, probably to use the lavatory. He reportedly heard a woman's voice say **"No,"** and a sound of something falling against the fence connecting the backyards of No. 27 and 29.

At 6 am, John Davis, an occupant of No. 29 Hanbury Street, prepared to go to his job for the day. His apartment was at the front of a three-story building that housed multiple families. It had a small backyard that easily connected to Hanbury Street via a 20-foot passageway, which meant that trespassers – including prostitutes and their clients – were frequent nuisances to the seventeen residents of No. 29.

The location of Annie Chapman's body

When he descended the stone steps into the backyard, he was met with a mutilated female body sprawled between the steps and the neighboring fence.

He noticed that her skirts were pulled up to her groin and, without further investigation, ran into the neighboring street to call for help. He flagged down three workmen, James Green, James Kent, and Henry John Holland, who took one look at the body and then rushed out to find a constable.

They soon came upon Inspector John Chandler of H Division on Commercial Street

"Another woman has been murdered," *they told him.*

Elizabeth Stride

September 30th, 1888; Berner Street, Whitechapel

Elizabeth Stride's body was discovered at about 1 a.m. on Sunday 30 September 1888 in Dutfield's Yard, off Berner Street (now Henriques Street) in Whitechapel.

Two distinct elements make Stride's murder unique among the canonical five. First, there were no mutilations to her abdomen in the way that there were on the bodies of the other four victims. Second, the cause of death was not determined to be strangulation, as there were no marks of strangulation on her body. The Ripper was clearly disturbed.

Elizabeth Stride's body at Dutfield'Yard

THE BRICKLAYERS ARMS 11.00PM ON SATURDAY 29TH SEPTEMBER 1888

EYE WITNESS John Best (Labourer)

The relevant extract from the Evening News reads as follows:

J. Best, 82, Lower Chapman-street, said:

I was in the Bricklayers' Arms, Settles-street, about two hundred yards from the scene of the murder on Saturday night, shortly before eleven, and saw a man and a woman in the doorway. They had been served in the public house, and went out when me and my friends came in. It was raining very fast, and they did not appear willing to go out. He was hugging her and kissing her, and as he seemed a respectably dressed man, we were rather astonished at the way he was going on with the woman, who was poorly dressed. We "chipped" him, but he paid no attention. As he stood in the doorway he always threw sidelong glances into the bar, but would look nobody in the face. I said to him "Why don't you bring the woman in and treat her?" but he made no answer. If he had been a straight fellow he would have told us to mind our own business, or he would have gone away. I was so certain that there was something up that I would have charged him if I could have seen a policeman. When the man could not stand the chaffing any longer he and the woman went off like a shot soon after eleven. I have been to the mortuary, and am almost certain the woman there is the one we saw at the Bricklayers' Arms. She is the same slight woman, and seems the same height. The face looks the same, but a little paler, and the bridge of the nose does not look so prominent.

THE MAN

The man was about 5ft. 5in. in height. He was well dressed in a black morning suit with a morning coat. He had rather weak eyes. I mean he had sore eyes without any eyelashes. I should know the man again amongst a hundred. He had a thick black moustache and no beard. He wore a black billycock hat, rather tall, and had on a collar. I don't know the colour of his tie. I said to the woman,* "that's Leather Apron getting round you." The man was no foreigner; he was an Englishman right enough.

EYE WITNESS John Gardner (Labourer)

From the Evening News article:

Gardner corroborated all that Best said respecting the conduct of the man and the woman at the Bricklayers' Arms, adding "before I got into the mortuary to-day (Sunday), I told you the woman had a flower in her jacket, and that she had a short jacket. Well, I have been to the mortuary and there she was with the dahlias on her right side of her jacket.

I COULD SWEAR

She is the woman I saw at the Brickayers' Arms and she has the same smile on her face now that she had then.

CHRISTIAN STREET 11.45 PM ON SATURDAY 29TH SEPTEMBER 1888

EYE WITNESS William Marshall (Labourer)

William Marshall living at 64 Berner Street testified to seeing a woman he later recognised in the mortuary as Elizabeth Stride. Three doors away he saw her standing with a man between Christian Street and Boyd Street at about 11.45pm.

Mr Marshall attention had first been drawn towards the couple because the man was kissing the woman, otherwise, he did not take too much notice of them.

He heard the man say

"you would say anything but your prayers"

Then they walked leisurely down the street. Neither appeared to be intoxicated.

THE MAN

He was middle-aged and stout, about 5ft 6in tall, respectably dressed in a small black cut-away coat, and dark trousers. He was wearing a small peaked cap, "something like a sailor would wear". He had the appearance of a clerk. The woman was wearing a black jacket and skirt and a black crape bonnet, but did not see the flower that was pinned to the jacket.

Marshall went inside at midnight and heard no more until a little after 1.00am when he heard the cry of "murder" being called in the street.

FAIRCLOUGH STREET 12.45 AM ON SUNDAY 30TH SEPTEMBER 1888

EYE WITNESS James Brown (Dock Labourer)

Witness at Elizabeth Stride's inquest.

Brown testified to seeing a woman with a man at 12.45am, 30th September 1888 in Fairclough Street whilst he was getting his supper from a chandler's shop on the corner with Berner Street.

He saw the couple standing by the Board School; the woman had her back to the wall, facing the man who had his arm up against it. Brown heard the woman say

"No, not tonight, some other night"

which attracted his attention. There was no trace of an accent in the woman's voice.

THE MAN

The man was described, as being about 5ft 7in tall and stoutly built, wearing a long overcoat which went down almost to his heels. He was wearing a hat, but Brown was unable to describe it. It was quite dark, so he could not tell if the woman was wearing a flower on her jacket, but both appeared sober.

Brown went home and finished his supper. Fifteen minutes later he heard screams of 'Police!' and 'Murder!', but on opening his window he could not see anybody in the street.

He told the coroner that he was almost certain that the woman was the deceased.

BERNER STREET 12.45 AM ON SUNDAY 30TH SEPTEMBER 1888

EYE WITNESS Israel Schwartz

In his report of 19 October, Chief Inspector Donald Swanson stated that Israel Schwartz, of 22 Helen Street, Backchurch Lane:

[At 12:45 am].. on turning into Berner Street from Commercial Road, & had got as far as the gateway where the murder was committed he saw a man stop and speak to a woman, who was standing in the gateway. He tried to pull the woman into the street, but he turned her round & threw her down on the footway & the woman screamed three times, but not very loudly. On crossing to the opposite side of the street, he saw a second man lighting his pipe. The man who threw the woman down called out, apparently to the man on the opposite side of the road,

*"*Lipski*"*

and then Schwartz walked away, but finding that he was followed by the second man, he ran as far as the railway arch, but the man did not follow so far. Schwartz cannot say whether the two men were together or known to each other. Upon being taken to the mortuary Schwartz identified the body as that of the woman he had seen and he thus described the first man who threw the woman down:

THE MAN

Age about 30, 5ft 5in, complexion fair, dark hair, small brown moustache, full face, broad shouldered, dress, dark jacket, trousers black, cap with a peak, nothing in his hand.

***Israel Lipski** (1865 – 21 August 1887) was a convicted murderer of Polish-Jewish descent living in the East-End of London

Catherine Eddowes

September 29th, 1888; Aldgate Street; City of London

At 8:30 PM on Saturday 29 September, City PC Louis Robinson saw a crowd gathered around 29 Aldgate Street. Approaching to see what all the commotion was about, he saw a woman lying in a heap in the center of the group of people.

"I asked if there was one that knew her or knew where she lived," he would later report, *"but I got no answer."*

Finding the crowd silent and the woman passed out drunk, Robinson enlisted the help of City PC George Simmons in getting her to her feet and dragging her to Bishopsgate Police Station.

Sergeant James Byfield was registering inmates when Simmons and Robinson brought the woman into the station around 8:45 PM. When Byfield asked her name, she replied, "Nothing." Five minutes later, she was placed in a cell, where she passed out. PC George Hutt was tasked with keeping an eye on the prisoners that evening, and passed by her cell several times as she slept.

An hour later, the City Police constables assigned to the night shift headed out through the gates of Bishopsgate Station to walk their beats. This included City PC Edward Watkins, whose fifteen-minute loop took him through Mitre Square, and

City PC James Harvey, whose route passed by Mitre Square at regular intervals.

At 12:15 AM, PC George Hutt heard the woman who was brought in earlier singing softly to herself in her cell. A few minutes later, she called out, asking when she would be released.

"When you are capable of taking care of yourself," replied Hutt.

"I can do that now," she said.

Several minutes later, she was finishing being processed, and amended her earlier registry of "Nothing" to Mary Ann Kelly of 6 Fashion Street. It was more believable, but still an alias. Her real name was Catherine Eddowes, sometimes called Kate Kelly. She was ready to be released by 1 am.

"What time is it?" She asked Hutt.

"Too late for you to get anything to drink," he replied.

"I shall get a damn fine hiding when I get home," she said.

"And serve you right, you had no right to get drunk," he admonished, opening the door for her. *"This way missus, please pull it to."*

She exited in the opposite direction of where her actual nightly residence had been, the Cooney's Lodging House located at Flower and Dean Street. Instead she headed back toward Aldgate High Street, where Robinson had discovered her earlier.

At about 1:30 am, Joseph Lawende, a commercial traveller, Joseph Hyam Levy, a butcher, and Harry Harris, a furniture dealer were walking nearby. They were heading down 16-17 Duke Street from the Imperial Club. The three passed by a couple walking in the opposite direction. Harris did not notice them at all, and Levy took little note of them other than the fact that they were both rather shabby looking.

Lawende, however, had the best memory of the couple's appearance of all. While he didn't see the woman's face, he was later able to recognize her clothing. He went on to describe the man as looking to be about 30 years old, five foot seven inches tall, with a mustache, wearing a loose-fitting salt and pepper jacket and a red handkerchief around his neck. Lawende was the last person, besides her killer, to lay eyes on Catherine Eddowes while she still lived.

Mitre Square was a ten-minute walk from Bishopsgate Station. Eddowes was discovered murdered there at 1:45 am by PC Watkins.

Catherine Eddowes murdered at Mitre Square

Mary Kelly

November 9, 1888; 13 Miller's Court, Whitechapel

When Bowyer arrived at 13 Miller's Court, he knocked on the door twice. Receiving no answer, he rounded the corner of the yard to see that a couple of glass windowpanes were broken. He reached in through the knocked-out glass and moved the curtain to see whether Mary Kelly was at home or not. The first thing he saw were what looked like two lumps of meat sitting on the bedside table.

13 Millers Court

The second thing he saw sent him running back to his employers' office. McCarthy followed him back to Miller's Court. He drew the curtain aside to see just what the office assistant had: a bloody corpse, mangled beyond recognition, with parts strewn all over the blood-soaked bed. McCarthy sent his assistant to find a constable, and Bowyer soon came across Inspector Walter Beck and Detective Walter Dew chatting on Commercial Street.

"Another one. Jack the Ripper. Awful. Jack McCarthy sent me."

Bowyer could barely get the words out of his mouth. The officers followed him, observing the carnage through the broken window with queasy horror. They sent for Inspector Abberline, who was in charge of the Ripper Case. The Inspector arrived at 11:30 am and Dr. George Bagster Phillips, a police surgeon who had also responded to the murder of Annie Chapman, arrived around the same time.

CHAPTER FOUR

THE LETTERS

> I'm not a butcher, I'm not a Yid,
> Nor yet a foreign skipper,
> But I'm your own light-hearted friend,
> Yours truly,
>
> Jack the Ripper.
>
> Anonymous

One of the first documents that Sir Melville MacNaghtem Assistant Commissioner (Crime) of the London Metropolitan Police from 1903 to 1913 perused at Scotland Yard from the numerous communications on the subject of the East End murders. He wrote about it in his book 'Days of My Years,' 1914.

> 'Up and down the goddam town
> Policemen try to find me.
> But I ain't a chap yet to drown
> In drink, or Thames or sea.'
>
> 'I've no time now to tell you how
> I came to be a killer.
> But you should know, as time will show,
> That I'm society's pillar.

Saucy Jacky postcard

(Transcription)

I was not codding dear old Boss when I gave you the tip, you'll hear about Saucy Jacky's work tomorrow double event this time number one squealed a bit couldn't finish straight off. Had not got time to get ears off for police thanks for keeping last letter back till I got to work again.

Jack the Ripper

25 Sept. 1888.

Dear Boss

I keep on hearing the police have caught me but they wont fix me just yet. I have laughed when they look so clever and talk about being on the right track. That joke about Leather apron gave me real fits. I am down on whores and I shant quit ripping them till I do get buckled. Grand work the last job was. I gave the lady no time to squeal. How can they catch me now. I love my work and want to start again. You will soon hear of me with my funny little games. I saved some of the proper red stuff in a ginger beer bottle over the last job to write with but it went thick like glue and I cant use it. Red ink is fit enough I hope ha. ha. The next job I do I shall clip the ladys ears off and send to the police officers just for jolly wouldnt you. Keep this letter back till I do a bit more work. then give it out straight My knife's so nice and sharp I want to get to work right away if I get a chance. Good luck.

yours truly
Jack the Ripper

Dont mind me giving the trade name

wasnt good enough to post this before I got all the red ink off my hands curse it No luck yet. They say I'm a doctor now ha ha

Dear Boss,

I keep on hearing the police have caught me but they wont fix me just yet. I have laughed when they look so clever and talk about being on the right track. That joke about Leather Apron gave me real fits. I am down on whores and I shant quit ripping them till I do get buckled. Grand work the last job was. I gave the lady no time to squeal. How can they catch me now. I love my work and want to start again. You will soon hear of me with my funny little games. I saved some of the proper red stuff in a ginger beer bottle over the last job to write with but it went thick like glue and I cant use it. Red ink is fit enough I hope ha. ha. The next job I do I shall clip the ladys ears off and send to the police officers just for jolly wouldn't you. Keep this letter back till I do a bit more work, then give it out straight. My knife's so nice and sharp I want to get to work right away if I get a chance. Good Luck.

Yours truly
Jack the Ripper

Dont mind me giving the trade name

PS Wasnt good enough to post this before I got all the red ink off my hands curse it No luck yet. They say I'm a doctor now. ha ha

Received on September 27th, 1888 at the Central News Agency

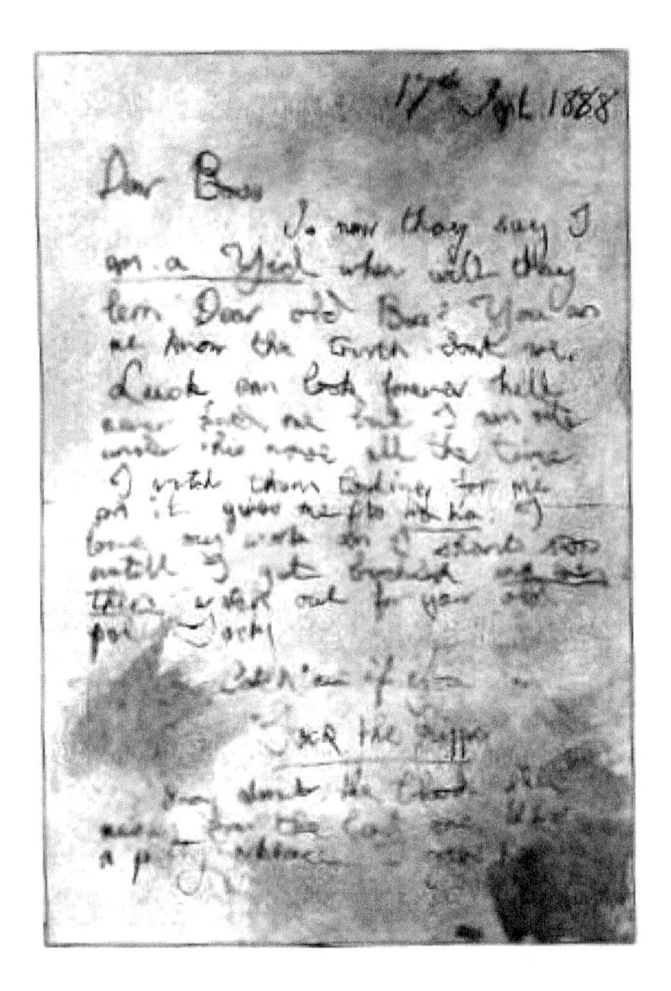

Here is another letter that taunts the Police by stating he is found right underneath their nose. He confuses us more he uses the name Jacky, the feminine of Jack as if to imply there

is an another accomplice a woman, 'I shant stop until I get buckled and even then watch out for your old pal Jacky.'

(Transcription)

17th Sept 1888

Dear Boss

So now they say I am a Yid when will they lern Dear old Boss! You an me know the truth dont we. Lusk can look forever hell never find me but I am rite under his nose all the time. I watch them looking for me an it gives me fits ha ha I love my work an I shant stop until I get buckled and even then watch out for your old pal Jacky.

Catch me if you Can
Jack the Ripper

Sorry about the blood still messy from the last one. What a pretty necklace I gave her.

From hell

Mr Lusk

　　　Sor
I send you half the
Kidne I took from one women
prasarved it for you tother piece
I fried and ate it was very nise. I
may send you the bloody knif that
took it out if you only wate a whil
longer

　　Signed Catch me when
　　　　　　　　　you can
　　　　　　Mishter Lusk

(Transcription)

From hell.

Mr Lusk,
    Sor
       I send you half the Kidne I took from one woman prasarved it for you tother piece I fried and ate it was very nise. I may send you the bloody knif that took it out if you only wate a whil longer

signed

Catch me when you can Mishter Lusk

Initially the Ripper letters was considered to be just one of many hoaxes, but when the body of Catherine Eddowes was found with one earlobe severed on 30 September, the writer's promise in the Dear Boss letter to "clip the ladys ears off" attracted attention. The Metropolitan Police published handbills with facsimiles of it and the Saucy Jacky postcard (which had referred to the earlier message and was received before the first became public knowledge) hoping someone would recognise the handwriting, but nothing came of this effort. Many newspapers also reprinted the text in whole or in part. These two messages gained worldwide notoriety after their publication. It was the first time the "Jack the Ripper" name had been used to refer to the killer, and the term captured the imagination of the public. Soon hundreds of other letters claiming to be from "Jack the Ripper" were received, most copying key phrases from these letters.

CHAPTER FIVE

THE SEARCH

The first deduction to make is the location of the murders. If we place those locations on the map perhaps we are given a clue. Indeed a simple mapping up of the scenes of crime locations of the murders at the time would of lead detectives to St Mary's Church. Since the first four first four deaths, draw the crucifix of Christianity. The intersection is with St Mary's Church. The location may have crossed the minds of detectives working on the case, but the conclusion would be unthinkable, inexcusable that a man of the cloth could even be considered as a potential suspect. It was of course this very thinking, that lead the Police astray. Even today in the minds of specialist researchers, that consideration has not even entered their minds. The first four locations draw us the crucifix of Christianity and that leads us to St Mary's Church.

MAPS OF THE WHITECHAPEL MURDERS

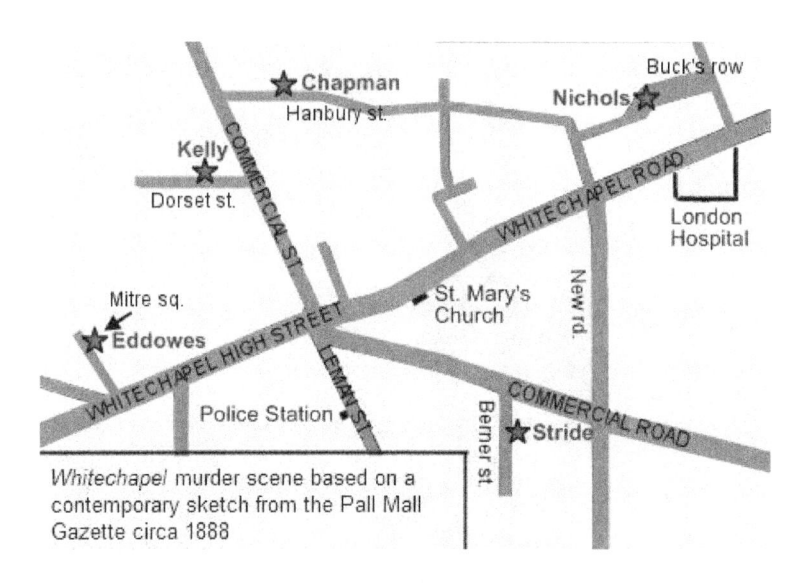

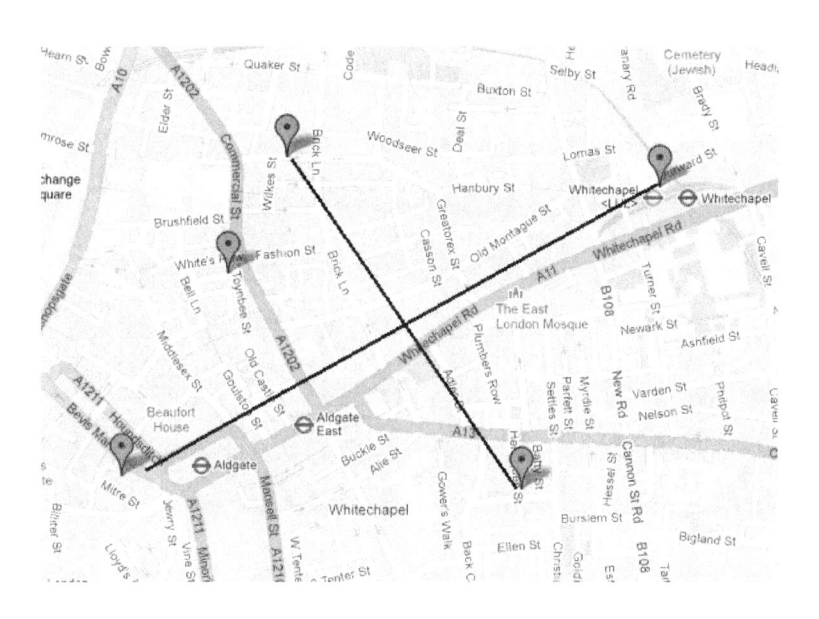

Whitechapel murder scene based on a contemporary sketch from the Pall Mall Gazette circa 1888

The first four deaths draw the crucifix of Christianity. Note: The intersection of the cross with St Mary's Church.

St Marys Church, Whitechapel, after the fire in 1880

Firstly, we are searching for a killer whose location points to St Mary's Church one who lives and works in that vicinity. The chalk marks and bloodied apron the two clues he left at Goulston St proceeding from Mitre Square are on route to this Church. .A curate perhaps, who would have a thorough knowledge of the streets and is at ease approaching an area amass with prostitutes. But more importantly exhibits odd behavior, that has attracted his superiors though they would not know, the inside workings of this killer 'Jack the Ripper.'

Documents are needed, as a witness and my research has found that in the annals of the Borough of Tower Hamlets a document dated 1895 written by a H.C.H. The document gives us a clue of the people operating at St Mary's Church. There is also a second document I found in the Australian historical archives a biographical account of a former curate.

THE FIRST DOCUMENT

An East End Vicar and his Work

Written circa 1895 by H.C.H

THE REV. G. C. DAW

Although a Londoner born and bred I am bound to confess that I was in painful ignorance of the precise locality of Spital Square until I had occasion to pay a visit to the Vicar of St. Mary's, the Rev. G. C. Daw. It is, therefore, not improbable that many of my readers may be in a similar position, and it will be well to state at once where it is and who are the people who dwell there.

Spital Square itself, as the street is called, is a turning out of Bishopsgate Street, and almost within sight, on the opposite side of the way, of the Liverpool Street Station extension, the terminus of the G. E. R. But the parish of St. Mary, Spital Square is, of course, of much wider extent. It includes two ancient 'liberties,' viz., those of Norton Folgate and of the Old Artillery Ground. These names call up some very interesting historical associations; but, as I ventured to remark to the good Vicar when I was chatting with him in his study one evening at the close of a long day's work, history is at a discount in a utilitarian age like the present, and it will be more to our purpose if we try to picture the parish as it is.

'You have some fine houses,' I observed to the Vicar, 'in Spital Square I thought yours was an East-end parish.'

'So it is,' he responded; 'you have seen the best of it the way you came in, but it will not be my fault if you don't see some of the worst of it as you go out. Yet even in Spital Square the houses are not tenanted as they once were. For the most part they are now let out in tenements, whereas a generation or so ago they were all occupied by good families, and one of them was a favourite resort of an English Sovereign.'

'But that was before the days of piano-organs,' I interposed, with a sly reference to one of those nuisances which I had noticed in full operation as I passed along, with a dozen or so boys and girls dancing round it.

'It was,' the Vicar rejoined; 'but you must not speak disparagingly of our only aristocratic quarter. As I said, we have a history, and we are proud of it. Do you not know that this parish was the home of the silk-weaving industry, and some of the best Spitalfields work was turned out from the looms here?'

'I do not doubt it,' I replied. 'But that must have been long ago.'

'Well, yes, it was,' the Vicar sighed; 'we have nothing of the sort here now. The weavers are all gone, and with them the old glory of the place has departed. We have one or two silk factories in the parish, but they are quite modern; and factory life at the East-end of London, even under the best conditions, is not what we should like it to be. You asked me what class our people belong to. We have a good number of factory hands, and of respectable artisans, but we have still more of the lower classes, such as market porters, dock labourers, costermongers, and the like. Our best *people dwell in the Norton Folgate part of the parish; but even there we have a few courts. The Old Artillery Ground, however, is now quite a poor district. The streets are small, and the houses in them are nearly all let out in single rooms, while the courts show a still lower order of things. Single rooms are a special feature of this part, and frequently we find a whole family huddled together in one room, the rent of which ranges from 2s. 6l. to 3s. 6d. a week.'*

'This must represent a very sad state of things,' I said.

'Yes, it does,' the Vicar sorrowfully replied; 'but,' he immediately added hopefully, 'our people are respectable, and there is very little immorality. Speaking generally, family life is held sacred here just as anywhere else. Our people are poor - some of them very poor - but our work amongst them is full of encouragement. If I were asked to describe the position here, I should at once say it was a decidedly hopeful parish.'

'You are not a stranger to East-end work?' I asked.

'Oh, no,' Mr. Daw replied. 'As a layman it was my privilege to work as a voluntary helper under the present Bishop of Bedford, Dr. Billing, when he was Rector of Christ Church, Spitalfields. Then in 1891 I was ordained, and my first and only curacy was with the Rev. E. A. B. Sanders, at Whitechapel Parish Church. I think, then, that I may claim to know something of the East-end, and I say that the work here is distinctly hopeful and encouraging. Of course, our parish is smaller than either Spitalfields or Whitechapel. But we have 5,000 people, and many of these are Jews.'

'Are you making any special efforts to seek these sons of Abraham?'

THE REV. H. F. MERCER

'Not at present; but I have plans in my mind which I hope may soon take shape. My work as Vice-Principal of the London Jews' Society College at Palestine Place - a post I held for ten years - has given me a keen interest in the welfare of the Jewish people, and it will be a great joy to me if I am permitted to bring some of my Hebrew parishioners to a knowledge of the Lord Jesus as the true Messiah. But special work of this kind requires time for its development, and as I have been here but little more than eighteen months I have had to spend much of the time in building up parochial machinery and organising the general work of the parish. My predecessor was a most devoted and saintly man, but he was left here too long, and with the growth of years his earlier energies naturally fell off. My desire has been to get hold of young people; I don't mean children only, but young men and young women, and I am much cheered by the results that have attended our efforts. I say 'our' because it would be quite impossible for any man single-handed to make an impression on this parish. Thanks to the C.P.A.S. this parish has enjoyed a grant for some years, and I have been able to have the services of a curate whose work here has been invaluable. I regret to say, however, that the clergyman I refer to, the Rev. H. F. Mercer, has just broken down in health, and I fear that the doctor will not allow him to return to East London work. But the point I want to make is this that the services of a curate in this parish are essential, and that without the help of the C.P.A.S. it would be impossible for that need to be supplied. I must, however, repeat that Mr. Mercer has been a most diligent and active worker. His open-air services in the summer were most successful, and I have reason to believe that they were greatly blessed to many. Then his Bible Class for young men has been a power in the

neighbourhood. He also took a deep interest in temperance work, and the Band of Hope has increased quite four-fold since he took it in hand. Another special department of his work has been the Church Lads' Brigade. He managed to get hold of some of the roughest lads of the parish. I am much disappointed that his health does not seem strong enough to bear the strain of an East-End parish. For strain it most certainly is. The visiting alone is enough to try even a strong man. You can imagine what it must be to spend a whole day going from room to room in these narrow courts. But it must be done. I know of no work more important than that of visiting the people in their homes. It gives us an influence over them that we cannot acquire in any other way. And it is most hopeful work here. I find it far less difficult than I did in Whitechapel. I can get into every room without the least hindrance, and I have never once been refused.'

Mr. Daw then suggested that we should have a look round the parish. It was getting late and I feared that there would not be much to see. 'Oh, we are late people in these parts,' he observed, and so it proved.

The light was still burning in the school room (St. Mary's is one of those parishes which, in spite of their poverty, are gallantly maintaining their voluntary schools), and we looked in. There, in one of the upper rooms, was the Mothers' Meeting just coming to a close. It seemed a strange time for such a gathering, but the women there assembled could not come at an earlier hour, for many of them had been at work all day.

A Bright Church.

From the schoolroom we passed into the church. It has lately been renovated and one could not but be struck by its bright and cheerful appearance. The walls and front of the galleries have been decorated in art colours, and the old-fashioned, high-back pews have given place to wide open benches. The Vicar has done well to make his church as bright and clean as possible, for there is too much that is dismal and dirty in the immediate neighbourhood. Asked about the congregations, he readily responded that they were increasing every week. When he first went there the church was but very sparsely attended, but the work in the parish is having its effect, and there seems reason to hope that before long the church will be comfortably full, at least at the evening service. The Vicar has secured grants from the S.P.C.K. and other Societies, and by these means is able to put a Bible, a Prayer-Book, and a Hymn-Book into the hands of every, one who comes into church. He uses the 'Numbered Prayer-Book,' and as the service proceeds announces the pages at which the different parts will be found -

the necessity for which is highly significant of the class of people attending the church.

Before bidding me good-night the Vicar piloted me through some of the smaller streets and courts of his parish. I found that they corresponded in every respect to his description of them - dark, dirty, and overcrowded - and I could well appreciate the force of what he said in reference to the trying character of a day's hard visiting in this neighbourhood. But there is light in the darkness, and one rejoices to know that the light is spreading. It is in such a field as this that the C.P.A.S. finds congenial soil, and its work there may, by God's blessing, be the means of turning a wilderness into a garden of the Lord.

THE SECOND DOCUMENT

Henry Frederick Mercer (1872–1949)

The next document I have found originates from Australia in an article written by John Tonkin which was published in Australian Dictionary of Biography, Supplementary Volume, (MUP), 2005.

Henry Frederick Mercer (1872–1949), clergyman and rogue, was born on 30 March 1872 at Barrow-in-Furness, Lancashire, England, son of Thomas Atherton Mercer, accountant, and his wife Mary, née Darricott. Educated at Giggleswick Grammar School, Henry entered Christ's College, Cambridge, in 1890, but remained only five terms. In 1893-94 he attended St John's College, Highbury (the London College of Divinity), and passed the Cambridge preliminary for theology in 1895. Made deacon that year, he served curacies in London (Whitechapel) and Hertfordshire.

GIGGLESWICK SCHOOL BUILDINGS

As a predominantly residential village, Giggleswick is most famous for its historic Grammar School, now an independent boarding school. The core of the village sits within a wooded 'bowl' on the western slopes of the Ribble Valley. It straddles the South Craven Fault which brings outcrops of sandstone and limestone together, reflected in the built environment.

The fault line also gave rise to Giggleswick Scar known as

*(**Buck**haw B**row**).

* Bucks Row the location of the first canonical murder in Whitechapel

H F Mercer attended Christ's College, Cambridge, in 1890. Before this date after leaving Giggleswick grammar school in 1888 he had time on his hands. I believe he used that time to come to London from his home in Lancashire to work for the, Church. I have searched the witness statements of the five canonical victims those that have been accepted as Jack the Ripper victims having the trade mark of the Ripper, but there are none, that state they saw a very young man, but there is the witness of a non canonical five victim who lived long enough to describe her attackers before she died the only one that had. She was Emma Elizabeth Smith *who became the target of a vicious attack in the early hours of 3 April 1888. Her murder possibly the first of the Whitechapel murders, and it is possible she was a victim of the notorious serial killer known as Jack the Ripper. Her account is given:*

Emma Elizabeth Smith

(c. 1843 – 4 April 1888)

At the time of her death in 1888 she was living in a lodging-house at 18 George Street (since renamed Lolesworth Street), Spitalfields, in the East End of London. She was viciously assaulted at the junction of Osborn Street and Brick Lane, Whitechapel, in the early hours of Tuesday 3 April 1888, the day after the Easter Monday bank holiday. She survived the attack and, although injured, managed to walk back to her lodging house.

She told the deputy keeper, Mary Russell, that she was attacked by two or three men, **one of whom was a teenager.**

Mrs Russell and one of the other lodgers, Annie Lee, took Smith to the London Hospital, where she was treated by house surgeon George Haslip. She fell into a coma and died the next day at 9 a.m. Medical investigation by the duty surgeon, Dr G. H. Hillier, revealed that a blunt object had been inserted into her vagina, rupturing her peritoneum. The police were not informed of the incident until 6 April when they were told an inquest was to be held the next day. The inquest at the hospital, which was conducted by the coroner for East Middlesex, Wynne Edwin Baxter, was attended by Russell, Hillier, and the local chief inspector of the Metropolitan Police Service, H Division Whitechapel: John West. The inquest jury returned a verdict of murder by person or persons unknown.

Emma Elizabeth Smith

Chief Inspector West placed the investigation in the hands of Inspector Edmund Reid of H Division. Reid noted in his report that her clothing was "in such dirty ragged condition that it was impossible to tell if any part of it had been fresh torn" Walter Dew, a detective constable stationed with H Division, later described the investigation:

As in every case of murder in this country, however poor and friendless the victims might be, the police made every effort to track down Emma Smith's assailant. Unlikely as well as likely places were searched for clues. Hundreds of people were interrogated. Scores of statements were taken. Soldiers from the Tower of London [which stood within H Division] were questioned as to their movements. Ships in docks were searched and sailors questioned.

Smith had not provided descriptions of the men who had attacked her (but one that one of them was a teenager) and no witnesses came forward or were found. The investigation proved fruitless and the murderer or murderers were never caught.

The case was listed as the first of eleven **Whitechapel murders** in Metropolitan Police files. Although elements of the press linked her death to the later murders, which were blamed on a single serial killer known as "**Jack the Ripper**", her murder was not thought connected with the later killings. With the exception of Walter Dew, who said he thought that Smith was the first victim of the Ripper. I am inclined to agree with it.

Analysis of facial cuts on Catherine Eddowes

What we do know about Jack is that he had a pathological hatred of women, a condition stemming from almost certainly from mother hatred. REV. H. F. Mercer's mother's name was Mary née Darricott, this is very important when examining Eddowes face, for he left deliberate markings on the face. We shall examine those marking's, the reader is first advised to study the name of his mother very carefully, the way it is spelt. Particularly the M, made up of two triangles for Mary. Note the middle name, née, and the glyph above the letter é, and finally the D of the alphabet for Darricott.

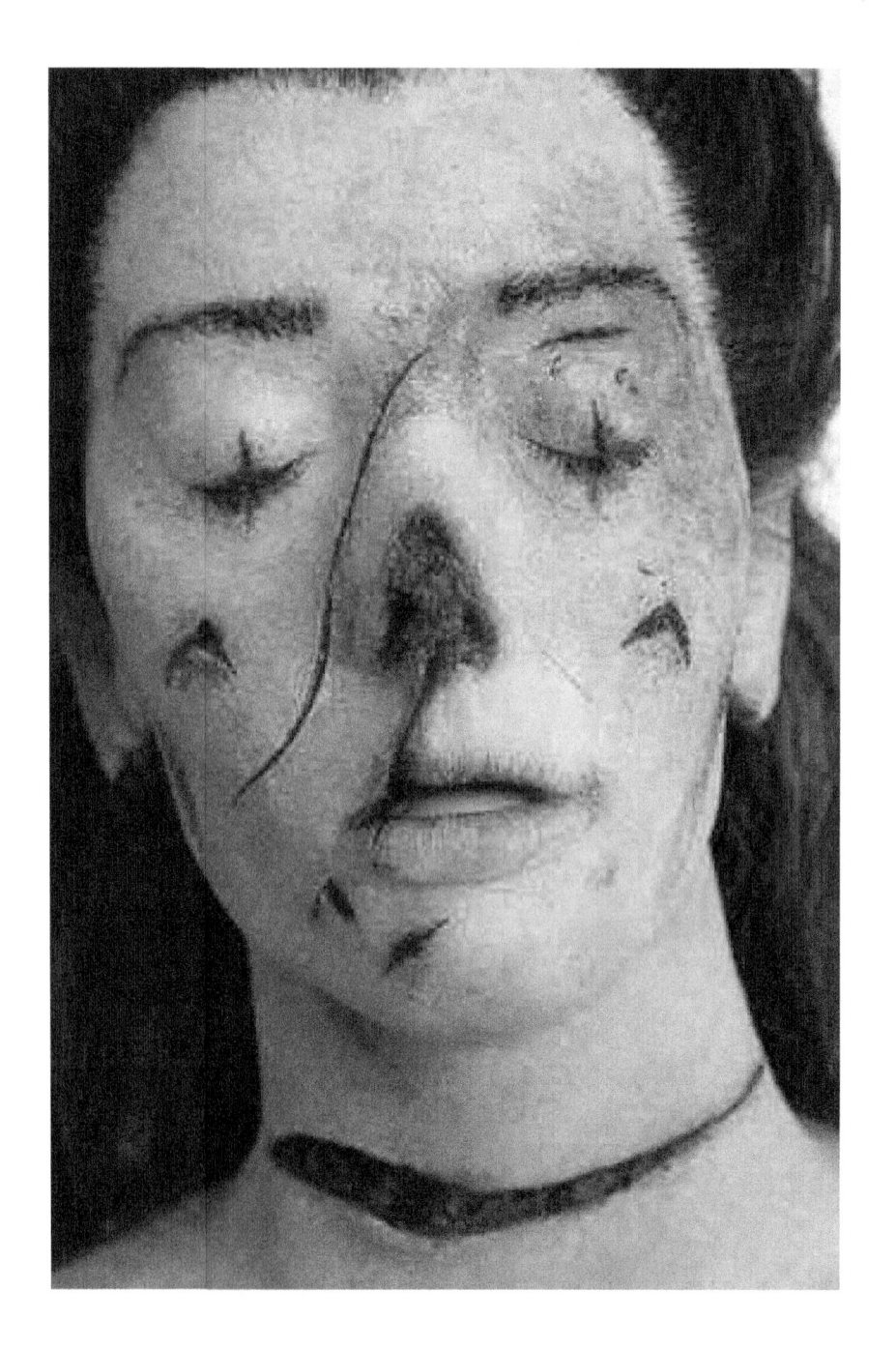

Catherine Eddowes

M First cut – Two triangular cuts on cheeks spell M for Mary

N Second cut – Nose cut spells N for nose

é Third cut - Left eyelid slit with glyph mark spells é for eye

e Fourth cut – Right eyelid slit spells e for eye

D. Fifth cut - Two stabs wounds to mouth plus two cuts to face making 4 cuts.
The fourth letter of the alphabet is D for Darricott

<u>SPELLS</u>

Mary née Darricott

The mother of H. F. Mercer

Sixth cut – Right earlobe cut off, meaning she never listened

Seventh cut to throat

THE REV. H. F. MERCER.

HENRY FREDERICK MERCER

Mercer a merchant who deals in textiles (i.e. knives)

I'm your own light-hearted friend,
Yours truly,

Jack the Ripper.

LIGHT (REV) – **H**EARTED **(Henry).** – **F**RIEND **(Frederick).**
–

JACK THE RIPPER **(Mercer)**

The use of 'hearted' has the initial H, for Henry. The use of 'friend' has the initial F, for Frederick. While the term Ripper could apply to his name trade of a Mercer. Mercers were formerly merchants or traders who dealt in textiles. The question is why did he give his first name as Jack, when his first name started with a H, for Henry. Possibly he used the name because Jack means: God is gracious. A reference to his future employment, one of the Church; time will show, a cleric, a pillar of society.

Eye witness Israel Schwartz heard the man shout 'Lipski, ' perhaps a derogatory remark, but the Ripper nevertheless could have resembled him, if a cap was placed on the head.

'Lipski, '

THE REV. H. F. MERCER.

H.F. Mercer

THE ASTROLOGICAL BIRTH CHART OF
REV. H. F. MERCER. BORN, 30TH MARCH 1872

Sun   Aries   9 degrees, Moon Sagittarius   12 degrees

Mercury Aries 26 degrees, Venus Pisces   11 degrees

Mars Aries 21 degrees, Jupiter cancer   20 degrees

Saturn Capricorn   20 degrees, Uranus Cancer 27 degrees

Neptune Aries 23 degrees, Pluto Taurus 18 degrees

A strong Aries fire sign he has four planets positioned here and this configuration is square in conflict with the position of Saturn in Capricorn at his birth. This configuration is a ticking time bomb. A look at the planetary ephemeris for the year 1888 reveals that during that whole year Uranus the planet of rebellion and freedom was travelling through Libra 17-21 degrees in retrograde the whole year. This transit would be in opposition to all the planets in Aries and also squaring his Saturn in Capricorn activating a mind of religious confusion. This transit would lead to high mental and physical tension, a breakdown in health resulting, in mental problems. High risks would be undertaken, injuries, cuts while travelling would occur indeed the ideal world he believed in was in reality not. Perhaps a religious ideal of heaven on earth, yet all around saw the depraved women, the drunkenness the promiscuity.

The year that followed 1889 he would suffer confusion to an even greater extent because Uranus transiting makes exact aspects to his planetary positions in Aries making the most powerful effect. While he committed his acts his actions back drop his growing confusion and this would get worse and so incapacitating him too carry out more of his murderous acts.

CHAPTER SIX

THE DISAPPEARANCE

Sir Henry Smith

Sir Henry Smith was educated at Edinburgh Academy and Edinburgh University.In 1885 he was appointed Chief Superintendent in the City of London Police Force.He was promoted to Commissioner of The City of London Police in 1890.During the time of the Whitechapel Murders, he was acting Commissioner of City of London Police.

Two decades after the murder of Eddowes, in his memoirs, Sir Henry Smith gave an account of witness Lawende that is evidently partially inaccurate. He called him "a sort of hybrid German", and gave - presumably from memory - another version of the description of the man he saw:

"Young, about the middle height, with a small fair moustache, dressed in something like navy serge, and with a deerstalker's cap - that is, a cap with a peak both fore and aft."

In his memoirs Smith wrote that the Ripper "...completely beat me and every Police officer in London." and that "...I have no more idea now where he lived than I had twenty years ago." (From Constable to Commissioner, 1910)

THE REV. H. F. MERCER.

Mercer, Henry Frederick (1872–1949)

On 12 May 1896 at St Saviour's Church, Bristol, he married Eleanor Kate Hill. He was ordained priest by the Bishop of St Alban's on 27 September 1896, and appointed to St Cuthbert's, Hampstead. The Mercers' daughter was born in 1897.

In 1899-1906 Mercer was metropolitan secretary of the Church Army in London then a student at Western University, London, Ontario, Canada, from which he graduated B.A. (1906) (and later falsely claimed to have an M.A.). On 7 February 1907 he was appointed to St Columb's Church of England, Hawthorn, Melbourne.

In 1909 was given special responsibilities for men's work. Mercer's wife died in 1908. On 2 August 1909 at All Saints' Church, Geelong, he married Victorian-born Jean Miller Tannock.

Mercer's reputation for bringing men back to the Church attracted the attention of Bishop C. O. L. Riley of Western Australia who installed him as dean of Perth on 15 April 1912. A good-looking man, fair-haired, 5 ft 10 ins (178 cm) in height and weighing about 11 stone (69.9 kg), he initially made a favourable impression. His stress on practical preaching and moral instruction matched Riley's interests well and he lost no time in introducing special services for men, supplemented by a mid-week social club (disbanded 1916) combining gymnastics with moral concerns such as opposition to gambling and promotion of temperance. These activities proved successful, though, according to the Truth newspaper, Mercer's observations on the temptations that men should avoid were 'so vaguely and delicately worded that any man might take his maiden aunt without fear of increasing the lady's stock of worldly wisdom'.

Meanwhile, serious doubts had developed about Mercer's character and Riley and the cathedral chapter came to believe they had been misinformed about his credentials. Moreover, by July 1916 the dean had contracted debts of over £2000, which were eventually paid by leading laymen, including Septimus Burt. A Truth columnist observed that 'Dean Mercenary was more a fool than a rogue'. Granted leave of absence on 8 September, he used the occasion to expand his earlier Citizen Military Force connexions to be appointed, on 28 September, chaplain (voyage only) in the Australian Imperial Force.

Mercer left Fremantle on 9 November 1916 in the troopship Argyllshire. Reaching England in January 1917 he was chaplain at No.2 Auxiliary Australian Hospital, Southall, London. He resigned as dean of Perth on 1 March and his A.I.F. commission in May. His wife and daughter returned to Melbourne where, in 1919, they unsuccessfully applied to the Department of Repatriation for a free passage to England. The family was never reunited. Jean Mercer was to die at Armadale, Melbourne, in 1947.

Mercer was a temporary lieutenant in the Royal Naval Volunteer Reserve from August 1917, and captain in the Royal Air Force in 1918-19. By 1921 he was teaching in an English school at Calcutta, India, styling himself 'Dr H. F. Mercer (late Captain A.I.F.)'. He was gaoled at Zürich, Switzerland, for twenty days in 1927 for failing to pay his hotel bill. In England between 1930 and 1948 he was imprisoned on five other occasions for periods of from six to eighteen months, for charges of minor fraud. From 1930 a woman said to be twenty years younger accompanied him; police attributed his problems mainly to 'the intemperate habits of the woman he calls his wife'. Mercer died on

22 February 1949 in Wandsworth Prison Hospital. An inquest returned a verdict of death by natural causes, the prison doctor testifying that 'he seemed to be a happy man and very cheerful up to within half an hour of his death'.

REV. H. F. MERCER age 44

OVERWISE KNOWN AS JACK THE RIPPER

THE END

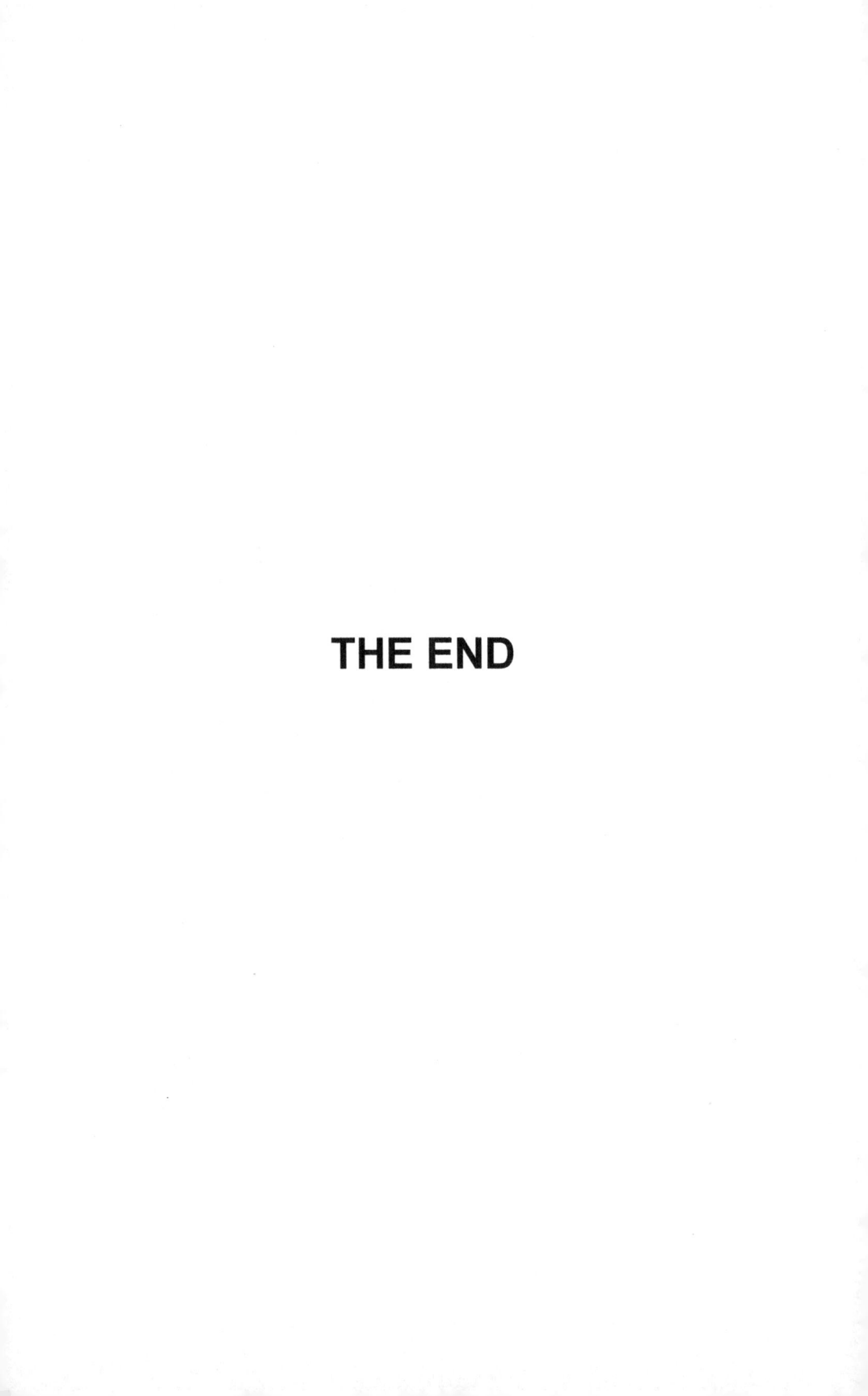